Mon

The Pock

KRZYSZTOF KIESLOWSKI

www.pocketessentials.com

First published in Great Britain 2000 by Pocket Essentials, 18 Coleswood Road, Harpenden, Herts, AL5 1EQ

Distributed in the USA by Trafalgar Square Publishing, PO Box 257, Howe Hill Road, North Pomfret, Vermont 05053

Copyright © Monika Maurer 2000
Series Editor: Paul Duncan

A CIP catalogue record for this book is available from the British Library.

ISBN 1-903047-25-0

9 8 7 6 5 4 3 2 1

Book typeset by Pdunk
Printed and bound by Cox & Wyman

Acknowledgements

This book could never have been written without the help of Film Polski and John Riley in acquiring videos of Kieslowski's earlier work, so thank you. Thanks also to Steve Kelly for getting me into this mess in the first place and to Paul Duncan for his endless patience and remarkable calm when faced with another missed deadline. To Ian Brook, whose sanity and perspicacity saw me through to the bitter end and to Sarah French who bore the brunt of it all, offering support and making herself scarce as she saw fit.

Contents

Krzysztof Kieslowski

"I'm somebody who doesn't know, somebody who's searching."

When Krzysztof Kieslowski died as a result of a heart bypass operation at the age of 54, people were shocked, but not surprised. The film-maker's own father had succumbed to tuberculosis at just 47 and Kieslowski, who had always suffered from weak lungs, also had a distinctly (un)healthy attitude towards his own fate, contentedly chain-smoking his way through life.

In fact, the film-making community was far more surprised when this prolific film-maker (he'd made over 20 hours of film in a single decade) had announced his retirement just two years earlier. He explained that he had run out of patience for film-making and for the fact that nothing turned out how he wanted it to, and that he planned to retire to his house in the country where he could read books, chop wood and, of course, smoke cigarettes to his heart's content.

Like the country he was born into, Kieslowski was never happily contained. Kieslowski was by nature a solitary smoker, sitting once removed from mankind. Behind a cloud of smoke, he could contemplate the paradoxes of fate and savour the ironies of human existence.

Poland, caught between Russia and Germany, had traditionally been the battleground between East and West, a country with a history of separation and exclusion. For Kieslowski, the Second World War - along with his father's ill health - contributed to an unsettled, peripatetic childhood. Later, under Communism, it was unthinkable that the individualist Kieslowski could ever be a Party member, but then he was too much of a cynical pessimist to please the firebrands of Solidarity either.

Even after 1989, when Communism collapsed throughout Eastern Europe and Kieslowski moved his film-making activities to France, he was a reluctant capitalist, protesting against the economic censorship of the West while retaining a nostalgia for the state-subsidised film industry of Poland's past. Like all great artists (although he would have cringed to be called so - he preferred the term 'artisan'), Kieslowski had a universal appeal while simultaneously being unclassifiable. Those who came across his later work considered him a mystical philosopher. Or perhaps obscure and pretentious. Those who knew his earlier work (Poles mostly) thought him a great humanist. A modern day maker of morality tales. Or even a traitor. Those who knew him personally thought him phlegmatic, modest, entertainingly cynical - and one of Europe's greatest auteurs.

"Really I make films because I don't know how to do anything else."

At first glance it seems unlikely that the same director who made, say *Workers '71*, an early documentary filmed after the strikes of 1970 and the downfall of Poland's progressive Communist leader Wladislaw Gomulka, and *Curriculum Vitae*, a short film about a Party control committee interrogating a fellow Party member and threatening him with expulsion, could have gone on to make a metaphysical poem such as *The Double Life Of Véronique*. Even more incredible that Kieslowski should claim that in all of his films he was aiming for the same goal.

But to understand Kieslowski it is vitally important to understand his background of documentary film-making. Throughout the 1960s and 1970s film - especially documentaries - played an important role in Communist Poland. The medium's impact was visual and direct, while an underlying, unspoken message often managed to elude the censors. Cinema - and documentaries were considered so important and were so popular that they were often made to be released on the big screen - became a social conscience for the people denied a certain way of living by the ruling powers. These were the precursors of the so-called Cinema of Moral Anxiety - a movement in Polish cinema, which strove to awaken social consciousness.

Although branded one of its leading lights, Kieslowski hated the term Cinema of Moral Anxiety. And just as naturally as the Cinema of Moral Anxiety developed from the documentaries of the 1970s, so Kieslowski's features developed from his own documentaries and then began to move away from the concerns of his fellow film-making compatriots. Even during his last films, Kieslowski claimed that he made features according to documentary principles: his narratives evolved through ideas rather than action. He even admitted, "I don't know how to narrate action" and, watching *The Scar*, a film about the building of a factory in rural Poland, you have to agree.

With his work, it was always the concept that came first: a series of films based on the Ten Commandments; a trilogy based on the notions of Liberty, Equality and Fraternity; a film examining the intangible essence of what constitutes a soul. Only after he (or more often his co-writer Krzysztof Piesiewicz) had come up with the original concept, could Kieslowski set about illustrating it. In the foreword to the collected screenplays of *The Decalogue*, Stanley Kubrick noted that Kieslowski and Piesiewicz had 'the very rare ability to dramatise their ideas rather than just talking about them.'

Kieslowski started out filming his features using techniques that he learned in his documentaries (in *Personnel*, the story of a trainee theatre dresser, documentary devices and techniques are employed to enhance a fictitious plot) and gradually integrated them deeper into his work. In fact, Kieslowski's work forms an incredibly coherent body of work, a trajectory heading in one direction, with each film taking the film-maker one step closer towards his ultimate goal. Themes are introduced in one film, then developed and refined in later ones. And despite the apparent differences in style between his earlier and later work, Kieslowski's concerns are to be found within a very narrow spectrum. They were concerns which, much to the chagrin of his Polish compatriots who so admired the Cinema of Moral Anxiety and who gave *No End* - an important departure for Kieslowski for it was the first of his films to touch upon the metaphysical with the introduction of a character who was a ghost - such a savaging, began to explore more fully the arena outside of politics. They thought Kieslowski had been unfaithful to his earlier ideals; that he'd given up on politics and documentaries. In one respect he had. The critical reception given to

No End, coupled with the introduction of a repressive Martial Law in Poland, left Kieslowski disillusioned with politics and finished with any representation of it on film. He also completely abandoned documentaries.

"A lot of people don't understand the direction in which I'm going," said Kieslowski. "They think that I've betrayed my own way of thinking, that I've betrayed my way of looking at the world. I really don't have any sense of having betrayed my own point of view, or even of having deviated from it, for whatever reason. I've been trying to get there from the beginning."

But where was Kieslowski trying to get to?

In retrospect, this reluctant film-maker was never happy with the medium of film. He considered literature a far more expressive form, but was convinced he couldn't write (even though he wrote, or co-wrote, all of his screenplays). And despite winning enough awards to keep even the most ambitious of directors happy, he was never content with what he'd made. Films were "stupid"; his chosen profession was "shameful and insignificant." The director was far more influenced by literature than he was by any other film-maker. He admired Ken Loach, and paid homage to him in *Camera Buff*, and also liked Fellini, Welles, Tarkovsky and Bergman, but he always claimed that it was the works of Shakespeare, Dostoyevsky, Camus and Kafka that shaped his own ideas. Notably, when he retired he claimed it would give him plenty of time to read books - never would he go to the cinema again! But perhaps Kieslowski's frustration stemmed from the fact that he'd set himself a nigh-on impossible task - to film the inner world, a world of emotions, of half-uttered meanings, of collisions of fate, was to attempt to capture the intangible. And he knew how difficult it was.

"The realm of the superstitious, fortune-telling, presentiments, intuition, dreams - all this is the inner life of a human being and this is the hardest thing to film. Even though I know that it can't be filmed however hard I try, the simple fact is that I'm taking this direction to get as close as my skill allows," he said. Modest as ever, he felt he didn't have the talent to attain what he'd set out to do, and besides, cinema was an inadequate medium for it. "The goal is to capture what lies within us, but there's no way of filming it," he said. "It's a great subject for literature. It's probably the only subject in the world. Great literature doesn't only get near to it, it's in a position to describe it." But Kieslowski was wrong. Cinema can get close to describing the inner world, and his cinema did. The sway of literature on his work was enormous, and not just because of his subject matter. Once his films are viewed in this light, and "read" almost as novels with their own internal narratives rather than movies along traditional Hollywood, or even independent, lines, the oblique moments - particularly in Kieslowski's later films - begin to make sense, opening up his characters' inner lives. Like great literature, Kieslowski's films can be interpreted and reinterpreted.

"Of course I'm playing on emotions. What else is there other than emotions? Only that."

If emotions or the inner life of someone are impossible to capture on screen, how did Kieslowski go about trying? He started with mood and atmosphere. Employing sensitive and creative cinematographers helped: Slawomir Idziak's expressionist style helped create the phlegm-coloured world of *Decalogue 5* and the tear-stained melancholy of *Three Colours: Blue*, invoking the right emotions from us before we even know which ones they're supposed to be. He found an eloquent and sparse composer in the shape of the surprisingly corpulent Zbigniew Preisner. And finally, he allowed his camera to delve into the inner, private world of his characters, to probe their minds and their non-thoughts: Véronique (*The Double Life Of Véronique*) experiences a wrench of pain when her Polish doppelgänger drops dead, and carries a light-refracting prism, a habit only she can explain; Julie (*Three Colours: Blue*) examines her reflection in the teaspoon used to sugar her coffee, drifts off and starts back to reality again to the sounds of her dead husband's unfinished symphony; Urszula (*No End*) plays a game with her dead husband while at the hypnotherapist's. All these express the most personal of moments which no one else is privy to. Save for Kieslowski.

It was his role of observer that leant itself so well to one of his *recurring themes:* observation and voyeurism. Filip (*Camera Buff*) obsessively records everything that moves with his new camera. Poor Tomek (*A Short Film About Love*) spies upon his neighbour Magda and sees her making love with another man while not even knowing Tomek's name. A despairing and impotent husband stalks his wife as she has an affair with a student (*Decalogue 9*). An infatuated Karol (*Three Colours: White*) shows his friend his wife's window and sees her in a silhouetted embrace. Auguste (*Three Colours: Red*) spies on Karin and sees her legs wrapped around another. Love, Kieslowski decided, is jealousy, it is unrequited, it means tears. Love means Dorota (*Decalogue 2*) adores two men, and is faced with an agonisingly difficult decision regarding her unborn child. Love encroaches upon a parent-child relationship in ways it shouldn't (*Decalogue 4*).

In the grander scheme of things, Kieslowski was preoccupied with the intersecting aspects of fate, destiny and chance. Call it a legacy - with his inherited weak lungs and Eastern European love of smoking, he was perhaps all too aware of his own fate. Call it environment - he was born into turbulent times where the wrong word to the wrong person could have you thrown in jail. Whatever the reason, he became a master of destiny. On celluloid at least.

One of Kieslowski's better-known earlier films, *Blind Chance*, depicted a young man, Witek, who was hypothetically thrust three ways depending on the outcome of a single event: whether or not he caught a train. The young man could become a Communist Party Member, he could become involved in the underground movement, or he could remain apolitical. While the various options of political life in Poland determined the film's subject matter, Witek's essential nature remained the same. He was not the puppet of fate; there was something greater than that determining what he was. It was also impossible to ignore the other, non-political, philosophical elements to the film - crossed wires, interwoven lives, the cruelly ironic workings of fate and chance and what Kieslowski called "a conditional mood of 'what if?'" - all of which were to feature with

12

increasing frequency in his later work. There is a sense of a greater orchestration at play, even if it is at the mercy of chance meetings and (un)happy accidents.

"An absolute point of reference does exist."

There is a strong spiritual force running throughout Kieslowski's films, and not just because of the chosen subject of his most ambitious work. Many people, no doubt because of his modern interpretation of the Ten Commandments, assume Kieslowski was religious. After all, he was brought up in a Catholic country. But for Kieslowski, this greater spiritual force was not God. At least, not in the traditional sense, for the film-maker hated organised religion as much as he hated any other organised movement (Communism, the army - even the fire brigade that he joined for three months as a school leaver!). But he did believe that "an absolute point of reference does exist... it's something which is lasting, absolute, evident and is not relative. And that's what a point of reference must be, especially for people like me, who are weak, who are looking for something, who don't know."

While making *The Decalogue* Kieslowski and Piesiewicz would constantly debate 'the truth'; what was right and what was wrong. Kieslowski was constantly searching for the answer. As well as being a collection of ten beautifully-written short films with not a scene or spoken line of dialogue out of place, *The Decalogue* is a product of this search - a stringently intellectual probing of moral dilemmas. Kieslowski had originally resisted attaching any specific Commandment to each instalment - and the title credits omit any reference, just giving a number - because he wanted viewers to work it out for themselves. He later bowed to pressure and tentatively allocated a Commandment to each instalment, but these could be easily cross-referenced or even interchanged. Without any prescriptive coda attached to them, they were designed to provoke their audiences into thinking about the issues raised as much as the film-makers had while making them.

In *The Decalogue* he asked difficult questions such as "What is Love?", "Who or what is God" and "Who guides us?" By the time he made his last film, Kieslowski seemed to have formulated some kind of a response with the creation of Joseph Kern, conductor of affairs in *Three Colours: Red*. Kern is an irascible and cantankerous voyeur whose mechanisms, although subject to the vagaries of fate, somehow manage to set those around him on the right course - although, of course, we have no guarantee that things will work out for them. Fate seems to be Kern's wild card, thrown in to make things more interesting. Some critics describe him as an omniscient, God-like figure. Kieslowski himself compared Kern to a chess player. Perhaps he was Kieslowski's closest representation of some kind of guiding force.

"Piesiewicz doesn't know how to write. But he can talk. And not only can he talk but he can think."

As so patently emerged with *The Decalogue*, Kieslowski viewed film-making as an essentially collaborative process. Which is why, if you read the published screenplays for either *The Decalogue* or the *Three Colours Trilogy*, you'll see they differ from the finished product. Kieslowski worked with Piesiewicz to draft the screenplays, which were then read by a group of fellow film-makers including Agnieszka Holland, Edward Zebrowski and Edward Klosinski. During filming, the cinematographer might have his say (so much so in the *Three Colours Trilogy* that the cinematographers each received a 'screenplay collaborator' credit) as would the actors. "If they're right, I agree with them," said Kieslowski simply. Even after he had edited *The Double Life Of Véronique* and screened the completed film he was happy to change the ending because American audiences didn't quite get it.

This collaborative means of working drew astonishing results in his musical partner, Zbigniew Preisner who he first worked with on *No End*. He liked Preisner precisely because of his willingness to collaborate. "Zbigniew is an exceptional composer,"

Kieslowski declared, "because he's interested in working on a film right from the beginning and not just seeing the finished versions and then thinking about how to illustrate it." The fruit of the partnership was not only a fictional 18th Century Dutch Composer, Van den Budenmayer (created by Kieslowski and Preisner for *Decalogue 9*, and whose music was so convincing that the Oxford University Press persistently wrote to Kieslowski demanding more details so they could update their encyclopaedia of music), but also the interweaving of music into the films as a narrative device rather than a theme or background atmosphere. For example, in *The Double Life Of Véronique* and *Three Colours: Blue*. The musical influences went even further, with some critics comparing the *Three Colours Trilogy* to a symphony in terms of rhythm, tone and range, journeying from grand opening to moving finale via a lighter, more carefree central sequence.

"I don't like the word 'success', and I always fiercely defend myself against it."

The supreme artistry at work in Kieslowski's later films, coupled with his choice of subject matter, did mean that the filmmaker's work approaches the complexity and variety of textual levels of his beloved literature. Typically, he would deny this. "When I film a scene with a bottle of milk," he explained, "somebody suddenly starts to draw conclusions which never even crossed my mind. For me, a bottle of milk is simply a bottle of milk. When it spills, it means milk has been spilt. Nothing more. It doesn't mean the world has fallen apart or that the milk symbolises a mother's milk which her child couldn't drink because the mother died early, for example. A bottle of spilt milk is simply a bottle of spilt milk. Unfortunately it doesn't mean anything else."

Are we to believe him? Surely someone who could tackle the complexities of a Commandment in just one-hour of screen time knew the importance of each second available to him? Here was someone who is forced to examine what is essential and what is not, and who enjoyed the editing process more than any other part of film-making (at one point he wanted to re-edit a new version for every French cinema showing *The Double Life Of Véronique*). Here was someone whose chosen ending to *The Double Life Of Véronique* was his heroine placing the palm of her hand on a tree - hardly an image lacking in symbolic weight. Despite his protestations and resistance to interpretation, Kieslowski was too much of an artisan, too much of a craftsman, not to be aware of that kind of symbolism. The answer is no, of course we don't believe him.

But it is precisely these tensions and contradictions that make Kieslowski - and his work - so fascinating. He denied that his films are symbolically loaded but they so obviously are. He attempted to film the unfilmable: ideas rather than actions, the inner life of human beings. He attempted to locate morals in the absence of God (a traditional one at least). Mood, texture and the inner life are key to understanding his films. Like his beloved literature, Kieslowski's films are open to be read on many levels. His advice would no doubt be to light up, kick back and have a think about it.

In The Beginning...

Krzysztof Kieslowski's birth - in Warsaw on June 27, 1941 - marked the start of an unsettled childhood. His father, a civil engineer, suffered from tuberculosis and consequently the family had a peripatetic existence moving from sanatorium to sanatorium. By the time Kieslowski was 14, the family had moved 40 or so times, something which the film-maker later remarked was excellent for awakening the curiosity. Kieslowski had poor lungs too, and would often stay at home reading - it was through books that he realised there was "something more to life than material things which you can touch and buy in the shops."

The first film Kieslowski remembered seeing was the swashbuckler *Fanfan La Tulipe* with Gina Lollobrigida when he was about eight years old. Although under-16s were not allowed, his parents had persuaded Kieslowski's great uncle, an eminent doctor, to arrange for their son to see it. Of course Kieslowski later recalled, "I remember absolutely nothing of the film." And although he claimed that he was never particularly fascinated with the camera, he did admit that, too poor to buy a ticket for the cinema, he would climb up to a roof and watch part of a screen through a vent and watch movies that way.

When he was 16, Kieslowski attended a fireman's training college but, hating the regime and the uniforms, lasted only three months. To avoid military school - which he was determined to do - the young Kieslowski had to continue with his studies. Another uncle of his happened to be director of a school for theatre technicians in Warsaw and so Kieslowski entered the Panstwowe Liceum Techniki Teatralnej with the intention of becoming a theatre director. Was it fate, or chance - just like the director would so often go on to probe in his films? Like Romek in his first feature, *Personnel*, Kieslowski became enamoured with the theatre. But he also admitted that had this uncle been a banker, he would just as happily have joined a bank.

Regardless, to become a stage director students required higher qualifications and so Kieslowski applied to Lodz film school.

Polish cinema as it was to become would have been unimaginable without this film school. Set up in 1948 Lodz attracted the brightest and the best. During Communism it was an island of freedom where students could see otherwise censored films and, after Stalin's death in 1953, the school flourished. But the school rejected Kieslowski. Twice. By the time he put his third application in (three years on from his original effort), he was no longer interested in a stage career, but his stubborn nature meant he wanted to get into the school simply because it had turned him down. Third time lucky, and whether it was fate or determination, Kieslowski spent a happy four years at Lodz.

Although he was inspired by the films of Fellini and Bergman, Kieslowski acknowledged that Ken Loach's *Kes* was the first to truly affect him. Indeed, Loach was the one film-maker who, he said, he would be happy to make the coffee for. "I always said that I never wanted to be anybody's assistant," Kieslowski said. "But that if, for example, Ken Loach were to ask me, then I'd willingly make him coffee. I didn't want to be an assistant or anything like that - I'd just make coffee so I could see how he does it all. The same applies to Orson Welles, or Fellini, and sometimes Bergman." From Fellini Kieslowski learnt a surreal poetry; from Bergman a probing rigor. And from Loach? His compassionate simplicity.

Two of Kieslowski's very first student films made in 1966 at Lodz indicated the two directions in which he would develop as a film-maker. The first was *The Office* (*Urzad*) a satiric documentary on the bureaucratic emphasis on rubber stamps while *Tram* (*Tramwaj*) was a fictional short that introduced the intertwining themes of romance and voyeurism when a young man catches a tram and stares at an attractive woman already on board.

The post-1968 period in Poland was a time of civil unrest and overwhelming disillusionment. A time when the ruling Communist Party began to clamp down on the move towards greater personal, social and artistic freedom which had been encouraged previously. Underground activities flourished and the public welcomed documentaries that seemed to show the life of ordinary Poles rather than any Party propaganda. To

Kieslowski, politically active as a student, it seemed natural to focus on making documentaries after graduation.

Many of these documentaries, unsurprisingly, depicted ordinary people working or fighting against state institutions. But Kieslowski always insisted that they were not intended as examinations of repressive regimes, but as portraits of the individuals.

Indeed many of them were just that. *I Was A Soldier* (*Bylem Zolnierzem*, 1970) is a talking heads documentary about men who lost their sight in the Second World War while *First Love* (*Pierwsza Milosc*, 1974) followed a young couple through marriage and the birth of their daughter. *Hospital* (*Szpital*, 1976) followed a group of orthopaedic surgeons on a 32-hour shift working in appalling conditions but retaining their humour, and *From A Nightporter's View* (*Z Pinktu Widzenia Nocnego Portiera*, 1977) was a sympathetic portrait of a fanatically right-wing factory worker. *Talking Heads* (*Gadajace Glowy*, 1980) asked 79 Poles, aged between 7 and 100, three questions: When were you born? What are you? What would you like most?

Increasingly though, Kieslowski realised that the very process of making documentaries, precisely because it invaded the individual's privacy, could never really depict true personal experience. Instead, he came to the conclusion that using actors and creating his own fictions would allow him greater access to the inner life of human beings and open up the full realm of their emotions. Added to this, an experience while making *Station* (*Dworzec*, 1980) put him off them for life. The police confiscated his reels of film and it was only later that Kieslowski discovered that a murder suspect had been in the station at the time he was filming. If Kieslowski inadvertently helped the authorities in their murder enquiries (he didn't; the suspect was never caught on camera) it would only be a matter of time before he would be helping them on a regular basis.

From that point, Kieslowski made the decision to concentrate on feature films.

Early Works

Pedestrian Subway (Przejscie Podziemne, 1973)

Cast: Teresa Budizsz-Krzyzanowska, Andrzej Seweryn

Crew: Direction Krzysztof Kieslowski, Screenplay Ireneusz Iredynski & Krzysztof Kieslowski, Cinematography Slawomir Idziak, TV, 30 minutes

Story: A teacher from a small town comes to see his estranged wife, a window dresser in the city, in the hope that she will return to him rather than go through with their divorce. They have a one-night stand before she pays him an unsentimental goodbye.

Curriculum Vitae (Zyciorys, 1975)

Crew: Direction Krzysztof Kieslowski, Screenplay Janusz Fastyn & Krzysztof Kieslowski, Cinematography Jacek Petrycki & Tadeusz Rusinek, TV, 45 minutes

Story: A Communist Party Control Committee cross-examines a Party member who has been threatened with expulsion. Although the man plays a role similar to one in his own life, the story of the accused is fictional - although the Party Control Committee is real. We never find out their decision.

Personnel (Personel, 1975)

Cast: Juliusz Machulski (Romek Januchta), Michal Tarkowski (Sowa)

Crew: Direction Krzysztof Kieslowski, Cinematography Witold Stok, TV, 72 minutes

Story: Romek, an idealistic 19-year-old, starts his new job as a tailor in the costume department of a theatre company. Enamoured with the arts, he is shown around and with naive enthusiasm takes in everything on his first day: from a massive prop of a horse being lowered outside in a courtyard to a pair of dancers rehearsing a pas de deux. He meets his new colleagues, one of whom, Sowa, is making a costume for a soloist, Siedlecki. After Sowa chastises Siedlecki for playing a practical joke on Romek with an exploding cigarette, the singer gets his own back by complaining to the opera directors that his costume is badly made. Sowa is then reprimanded at a worker's meeting where, instead of defending himself, he argues that the theatre's problems go beyond badly-made costumes, claiming it stages old plays to half-empty theatres. Romek meanwhile suggests that the technicians put on their own cabaret as a way of expressing themselves. One of the theatre chiefs then takes Romek aside and offers him help in finding an apartment and with his studies. In this scene Romek can be seen wearing a new pair of glasses. In the final scene, Romek is summoned by the director of the opera who asks whether it is true that Sowa encouraged the drinking of vodka at work. The director asks him to write down the details of the Sowa/costume incident. Romek initially tests his pen, but then replaces its lid.

Background: By 1975 Kieslowski had become interested in the idea of combining the documentary skills that he had already acquired with drama. He noticed that when he made documentaries much of the material he threw out consisted of people's observations or gossip, and that he rather liked these out-takes and was sorry to see them go. "When people started talking about this and that in a way which was amusing and moving, the documentary would grind to a halt because the idea behind it had stopped unfolding," he said later. "And then I thought that I'd use this sort of material as a dramatic device." The result of this was *Personnel*, Kieslowski's first feature-length film, made for Polish TV. Using real tailors at the Wroclaw Opera, much of the footage was improvised with Kieslowski giving the cast members topics for discussion and just letting the cameras roll.

Comment: Although Kieslowski wanted to acknowledge his thanks to the school for theatre technicians where he studied, and also to the Teatr Wspolczesny where he worked as a dresser, the director saw the context of theatre and opera as a metaphor for life in Poland: "It's obvious that the film is about how we can't really find a place for ourselves in Poland. That our dreams and ideas about some ideal reality always clash somewhere along the line with something that's incomparably

21

shallower and more wretched." Nevertheless, *Personnel* is perhaps Kieslowski's most autobiographical film.

Along with two shorter fiction features that he had already made, *Curriculum Vitae* and *Pedestrian Subway*, *Personnel* constitutes Kieslowski's transition from the documentary description of external reality to an exploration of people's interior possibilities. But the documentary style remains: a hand-held camera follows the minimal action, with a loose and free style of cinematography that feels ultra-naturalistic. What is being observed here are people's faces, their minds, hands and behaviour. The emphasis is very much on Romek's gaze as he watches everything from props being moved and scenery being prepared through to the final performance. And what Romek, like Sowa before him, learns is that his lofty ideals about art are an illusion: Theatre is a gossipy, machiavellian, political and dangerous business. The directors of Romek's theatre consider their young recruit still naive enough to be bought and they offer help in return for information. But if he writes down the details as required by the opera director, Romek will have sold himself and betrayed his mentor and friend Sowa. If he refuses, he will forfeit access to privileges which the system offers before he has even had a chance to establish himself.

Images: Mirrors and glass. In the opening sequence of Romek's arrival, his reflection is shown seven times in a series of stationary and moving mirrors. Not only is Kieslowski indicating to us that this story is a reflection of more than just the theatre (which is itself a window on the world), but the moving mirrors indicate the shifting of Romek's perception that will take place. With the emphasis on Romek's gaze, we see him constantly looking through windows to observe what goes on behind the scenes. All these images culminate with the pair of spectacles - enabling clear vision - that Romek wears in the last few scenes.

Recurring Ideas: A scene in which Romek runs to catch a train is shot in a way that prefigures *Blind Chance* and the central scene of Witek running for the train. And already Kieslowski shows his predilection towards a red (the theatre carpet), white (theatre walls) and blue (lighting, and the cutters'

22

overalls) colour scheme which would figure in the *Three Colours Trilogy*.

Verdict: Intriguing, but a weak narrative. 2/5

The Scar (Blizna, 1976)

Cast: Franiszek Pieczka (Stefan Bednarz), Jerzy Stuhr, Maruisz Dmochowski

Crew: Direction Krzysztof Kieslowski, Screenplay Romuald Karas & Krzysztof Kieslowski, Story Karas, Cinematography Slawomir Idziak, Feature film, 104 minutes

Story: At a patently corrupt Party meeting, a decision is made to build a new chemical plant in Olecko, a depressed rural town. Well-meaning Party man Stefan Bednarz is sent to Olecko - where he lived 20 years ago with his wife before leaving after an embarrassing, unspecified incident - to oversee the construction and running of this large plant. While the bureaucrats say that the plant will invigorate the local economy, the area's inhabitants prove to be vociferously opposed to having their homes bulldozed and their forests cut down. In the process of dedicating himself to running the chemical factory, Stefan sacrifices his marriage and his relationship with his daughter, who later becomes pregnant. Furthermore, over the course of the years, the facilities promised by the Party fail to materialise. In the face of continued local opposition coinciding with unrest in the Gdansk shipyards and with the growing realisation that his faith in the project was misplaced, Stefan tries to resign, but is forced to stay until fired. In the closing scene we see Stefan teaching his grandchild to walk.

Background: Kieslowski's first theatrical feature was also the first of only two of his films (the other was *Short Working Day*) that was developed from previously published material rather than an original idea or concept. Although Kieslowski based this film on a report by journalist Romuald Karas (who also co-wrote the screenplay), he added his own action, plot and characters, later admitting that he "did it badly." Nevertheless *The Scar* marks an important transition for the director, moving on

23

from *Personnel* and depicting through the course of its action a move from the political to the personal.

Comment: The Scar displays elements of the documentary style that Kieslowski had so far developed. This can be seen in the scenes in which crowds gather for the opening party for the plant or the meeting that the plant holds with the townspeople. But *The Scar* also looks ahead to his later work, showing a level of poetic stylisation and some virtuoso shots: when Stefan arrives in the town there is an extended, sideways sweeping shot; when he first enters his flat he switches the light on and off, being reflected in the window or seeing through to the gorgeous landscape outside at the flick of a switch. Tragedy is conveyed with the burning of the forest while the men in suits prove comically incongruous in the wild forest locations. As in *Camera Buff*, a protagonist is compromised by political pettiness and finally redeemed by looking inward. There is much emphasis on 'truth' (the journalists and sociologists who chart the course of the plant and the authorities attempt to conceal it) and its associated dangers.

Verdict: Too political, too dull. Kieslowski was right - he can't narrate action. 1/5

The Calm (Spokoj, 1976)

Cast: Jerzy Stuhr (Antek Gralak), Izabella Olszewska, Jerzy Trela

Crew: Direction Krzysztof Kieslowski, Screenplay Krzysztof Kieslowski & Jerzy Stuhr, Story Lech Borski, Cinematography Jacek Petrycki, TV, 70 minutes

Story: Antek Gralak is released from prison after serving three years of a five-year sentence. He starts a new construction job and rents a room and, while out drinking and dining with his new colleagues, tells them that all he wants is peace and quiet: a wife, kids, his own place, enough food to eat and a television. Nothing more. On returning home he gets frisky with the landlady, but has drunk too much vodka for anything to happen. Later he revisits some acquaintances and is attracted to the daughter of the family, whom he subsequently marries. When cement and bricks disappear from the work site and the boss deducts the loss from the workmen's wages, the men decide to strike. The boss thinks that because of his background Antek's co-operation can be bought, but on meeting resistance to this is eventually forced into blackmailing Antek with the suggestion that he will be the police's prime suspect in the theft. Antek tries to mediate with the boss, but the men feel that he has betrayed them and they beat him up. As they run off, Antek is left behind repeating: "Calm" through his bloody mouth.

Background: After casting a then-unknown Jerzy Stuhr in *The Scar* (in which he played an insidious official), Kieslowski decided that he wanted to continue the collaboration. "I absolutely had to make a film specially for him, so *The Calm* was made essentially for Stuhr," he said. The film was made during a tumultuous year in Poland, a year that saw workers' strikes and the formation of the Komitet Obrony Robotnikow (The Worker's Defence Committee), the first opposition of any kind the authorities had seen since the war. And because *The Calm* depicted a strike on screen for the very first time, the film was perceived by the authorities as a threat and summarily shelved. By the time it was released a few years later, Kieslowski declared it "a period piece."

Comment: Although Kieslowski later claimed that "*The Calm* hasn't got anything to do with politics. It simply tells the story of one man who wants very little and can't get it," the film's censorship caused many to interpret it as having a revolutionary message. All Antek wants is: "A job, a place to sleep, food to eat, a family." And Kieslowski's message seems to be that even Antek's most basic needs are not within his reach. Antek is caught in the middle of a dispute: he wants the approval of his peers, but is grateful to his boss for employing him despite his criminal record (although, as in *Personnel*, the higher authorities think that the protagonist can be bought). Just as in Kieslowski's subsequent *Blind Chance*, the film-maker implies that you will not survive if you refuse to take sides.

Images: Horses. First seen as an image transmitted through a television test signal, galloping horses, representing the freedom that Antek cannot achieve, are seen again when Antek is on the night bus and once more after he is beaten up. Antek also imitates the sound of galloping hooves with his hands at his wedding.

Recurring Images And Ideas: Mirrors. There is one virtuoso scene involving a mirror in *The Calm*. Antek is getting dressed to go and visit his boss and facing the camera. When he turns to walk out of the room we realise the camera has been in the place of the mirror and the angle of vision, just like Antek's loyalties, is suddenly shifted. The ending, with Antek repeatedly shouting one word, is again used by Kieslowski in *Decalogue 5*.

Verdict: The first real collaboration with Stuhr, who is great in an otherwise mediocre film. 2/5

Camera Buff (Amator, 1979)

Cast: Jerzy Stuhr (Filip Mosz), Malgorzata Zabowska (Irka), Ewa Pokas (Anna), Stefan Czyzewski (Director), Jerzy Nowak (Osuch), Tadeusz Bradecki (Witek), Krzysztof Zanussi (Himself)

Crew: Direction Krzysztof Kieslowski, Screenplay Krzysztof Kieslowski & Jerzy Stuhr, Cinematography Jacek Petrycki, Feature film, 112 minutes

Story: Filip, a young man whose wife is pregnant, buys an 8mm camera in anticipation of the birth of his first child. Soon however, he goes beyond the filming of his domestic surroundings and is asked by his factory boss to record the company's 25th anniversary. Filip ends up submitting the result to an amateur film festival, where he wins third prize. To the concern of his wife, he becomes increasingly obsessed with recording the world around him - from his neighbours to the daily goings-on in his street. His next project is to make a documentary about a co-worker; his boss agrees, but only if the company has script approval. The authorities are angered when they find out that the documentary is about a handicapped worker, but Filip allows the end result to be broadcast on television regardless. He then decides to become an investigative journalist, thinking he will expose corruption by showing a building that was begun with money from a grant and later abandoned. His 'hobby' costs him not just his wife (who leaves him while pregnant with their second child), but he discovers that his actions have resulted in the sacking of a colleague and could endanger the jobs of others. Distraught, he exposes the last spool of film he shot. Finally, he turns the camera on himself, and begins to narrate his own story.

Background: Although Kieslowski denied that the character of Filip was based on himself, the director was a self-confessed camera buff who once used the same make of camera (Krasnogorsk) that Filip buys. Like Filip, Kieslowski also started out by making documentaries and later claimed: "there were many documentaries which I didn't make. I managed to put a few of them into *Camera Buff*... A documentary about pavements, or about a dwarf. Filip makes them." Like his protagonist, Kieslowski also rejected the documentary form of film-making, and for similar reasons. When the militia confiscated some footage that the director had shot at Warsaw Central Station, Kieslowski dropped an activity that could, however unwittingly, potentially aid the powers that be.

Comment: At the start of the film, Filip has achieved what Antek in *The Calm* so longed for: a home, family, even a television. But he soon discovers this is not enough, and *Camera Buff* depicts the rites of passage of the budding film-maker. Starting out as a mere cameraman, Filip begins by just recording everything around him. Soon, however, he graduates to directing (Filip's request to re-enact his baby's homecoming which he forgot to film the first time round is rejected by his wife, although he has better luck directing a pigeon by luring it back to the window ledge with some bread crumbs). After he has filmed his company's anniversary celebrations, he is told to add commentary and music to his footage, and learns the skills of editing. But when his boss orders him to cut some scenes from the film, he is faced with censorship; similarly when he suggests a documentary on one of his co-workers, it is agreed to by the authorities, but only on condition that they have script approval. Then, when Filip travels to the film festival, he not only comes into contact with the pretensions and the politics of 'art,' but he also comes into contact with Polish director Krzysztof Zanussi (the head of Kieslowski's production playing himself in this film) and learns the political and social responsibilities of film-making. (Incidentally, Zanussi empathises with Filip having to have his script approved: "Someone always has to approve scripts. Mine too" – a pertinent comment on all film-making whether in Communist Poland or Hollywood.) It is only after Filip's well-intentioned films result in the sackings of several co-workers does he realise he cannot shoulder the responsibilities that his camera brings.

In the last scene we see Filip come full circle, turning the camera on himself and recounting his tale, becoming a story-teller. Perhaps Kieslowski is suggesting that only with self-knowledge does Filip now have all the skills necessary to be a truly effective film-maker.

Images: Birds. The opening sequence in which Filip's wife Irka dreams of a dark hawk attacking white chickens implies that we are about to enter a Darwinian universe. How does a film-maker fit into this? And will Filip be a survivor?

Mirrors and glass. Filip comes home to discover that Irka has smashed the mirror in their hall - a premonition that Filip's film-making will destroy their life together. Another time he comes home to find Irka has locked herself in the baby's room - the frosted glass in the door that separates them prevents them from seeing each other clearly, suggesting not only that they cannot communicate, but that neither of them can see the whole picture.

Circles. When Filip finally turns the camera on himself, we see the circle of the lens - by starting to tell his story from the beginning, he has now come full circle.

Look Out For: Keep an eye out for Kieslowski's homage to one of the few directors he admired – Ken Loach – when Filip thumbs through a book on film-makers.

Verdict: Kieslowski's first masterpiece. 4/5

Short Working Day (Krotki Dzien Pracy, 1981)

Cast: Vaclav Ulewicz

Crew: Direction Krzysztof Kieslowski, Screenplay Krzysztof Kieslowski & Hanna Krall, based on Krall's *View From A First Floor Window*, Cinematography Krzysztof Pakulski, TV, 79 minutes

Story: The film opens with three pivotal scenarios. In 1968, a young man addresses a meeting by denouncing the 'firebrands' who are agitating Warsaw students; we then jump forward to 1975, and the same young man is appointed First Secretary of the Communist Party; flashforward again to 1981, and on television the secretary is explaining his actions during "the events of five years ago." *Short Working Day* then segues into the events of June 25, 1976, a day on which the Polish people revolted in response to the government's 69% increase in the price of meat. Through a description of external events and the Party secretary's internal monologue, Kieslowski charts the day from 6am, when word of the protest first reaches the secretary, until 2pm, when the workers storm the building, forcing the secretary to evacuate.

Background: Unlike *The Calm*, Kieslowski set out to make an explicitly political film with *Short Working Day*. What the two films did share, however, was the same fate at the hands of the censors. But even when the ban on *Short Working Day* was lifted, Kieslowski refused to show it, calling it "a terrible film." His explanation was that it was a "film of its moment which, had it been shown at the time, might perhaps had have some significance, but not necessarily... It has not been shown to this day - fortunately."

Comment: The shortcomings of *The Scar* recur five years later in *Short Working Day*, which is based on the real events of June 25, 1976. Much of the action is non-action: an angry crowd gathers and a Party Secretary worries about how to deal with the situation, mediating between the crowd outside his local Party office and the intransigent authorities at the other end of the phone in Moscow. Like Antek Gralak (*The Calm*) and Filip Mosz (*Camera Buff*) before him, he is caught in the middle of two opposing forces. Except, unlike Gralak and Moscz, he is presented in a critical light. "I suspect that the film didn't work because in the script we didn't try hard enough to understand the main character," said Kieslowski. "I had set myself a trap because in Poland at that time there was absolutely no question of the public wanting to understand a Party Secretary."

Images: Erm...none that I can see. Stylistically, the main technique of interest is Kieslowski's choice of picking out certain characters in freeze-frame and then giving us a glimpse of what lies ahead, before cutting back to the main action. The first is a bearded man whistling in the crowd; after the freeze-frame we see him being arrested and beaten by the militia. Next is a woman who thrusts her paycheque in the secretary's face demanding how to live on her paltry salary; then we glimpse her at a trial where she is sentenced for "hooligan behaviour." Although these suggest something positive for the secretary and the authorities, the fate of the next three frozen faces implies a change in political tides. A man with curly hair is caught while pulling down a party slogan in the street; the flashforward cuts to young man telling his wife that his group will help pay for a lawyer. Next is a man with a moustache in the secretary's office; we cut forward to scenes of him celebrating the radio announcement that an agreement has been signed with the Gdansk ship workers. Finally a young man building a barricade in the street is stopped in mid-action; we see him later broadcasting on the radio on behalf of Solidarity.

Verdict: "It's boring, badly directed and badly acted... I've absolutely no idea why I made it." 0/5

Blind Chance (Przypadek, 1981)

Cast: Boguslav Linda (Witek), Tadeusz Lomnicki (Werner), Boguslawa Pawelec (Czuszka), Monika Gozdzik (Olga)

Crew: Direction Krzysztof Kieslowski, Screenplay Krzysztof Kieslowski, Cinematography Krzysztof Pakulski, Feature film, 122 minutes

Story: Set during the heady political climate in Poland of the late 1970s, young medical student Witek asks the dean of his school for a sabbatical following the death of his father. He runs at full speed for a train. Tension mounts. Will Witek catch the train? Kieslowski presents us with three hypothetical outcomes. In the first, Witek boards the train, meets dedicated Communist Werner, and joins the Party. He bumps into his first love, Czuszka, who is a member of the underground movement, and they rekindle their affair. When Party bosses send him to stop a revolt at a hospital where the patients have locked up the doctors and taken over the wards, Witek tries unsuccessfully to mediate between the patients and the authorities. On his arrival home, Czuszka is arrested and interrogated by the authorities, and afterwards rejects Witek. Dispatched to a meeting in France, Witek is told he cannot leave because of the strikes in Poland.

We then cut back to Witek running for the train again. In this second re-enactment, the young medical student misses the train and fights with a station guard. Sentenced to community service, he meets Marek, who introduces him to the underground movement. Through Marek, Witek also meets a priest, Stefan, and is baptised. He starts an affair with a married Jew, the older sister of his friend Daniel, who 'emigrated' to Denmark when they were children. Witek is sent to the home of a woman who has just been raided by government thugs. She tells him that she is afraid of nothing and that life is a gift. The underground movement's samizdat printworks are also raided and Witek is spurned by his colleagues who hold him responsible. Witek, who wants to go to France for a meeting of Catholic Youth, is told by the authorities that he will be given a passport only is he gives them names, which he refuses to do. On returning home, his aunt tells him about the strikes.

In the third and final section Witek misses the train again, except this time he bumps into his student friend Olga and they strike up an affair. He resumes his studies and is asked to stay on after graduation to conduct research. He and Olga marry and have a child. Witek refuses to join the Party, but he also resists religion and signing dissident petitions. When the dean of his school asks Witek to take his place at a medical conference abroad he agrees, but changes the flight so he can be with Olga for her birthday. His new flight is via Paris. Shortly after take-off, the plane explodes.

Background: Only after Kieslowski had shot and edited around 80% of *Blind Chance*, did the film-maker realise that he was unhappy with the material he had. "It was mechanical," he complained. He gave himself a break of two or three months from the film, something he often did in order to give himself, as he called it, "a certain margin of freedom." Even after he went back to it and completed it, Kieslowski still wasn't happy with the end result. "I think its fundamental flaws lay in the script, as usual," was his judgement. "I like the idea to this day; it is rich and interesting. I just don't think it was made use of."

Comment: Kieslowski is perhaps the most severe, but also the most perceptive, critic of his own work. The idea is indeed intriguing, but somehow it just fails to gel. In *Camera Buff*, the hero had turned the camera on himself, and *Blind Chance* is Kieslowski's extension of this. While the premise is set up by three differing outcomes of a single event, *Blind Chance* moves away from describing an external reality, and instead focuses on the inner world. Witek's essential honesty is manifest is all three segments, regardless of his political or religious stances. Choice is not necessary - underlined by Witek's dying father's words: "You don't have to do anything" – to define one's personality. A decent and honest person can live decently and honestly on both sides. The course of Witek's life may be at the mercy of fate, but his essential nature is not determined by chance.

Images: The entire film unfolds under Witek's disturbing scream of "No!" Only at the very end do we realise that it is his scream on the plane. The shot moves into Witek's open, terrified mouth and we are presented with another 12 images of Witek's life - real or imagined. These include what seems to be the hospital aftermath of an accident (possibly the plane crash), with dead bodies on the floor while one is pulled along leaving a streak of blood. They also include Witek's goodbye to his childhood friend, Daniel, who is emigrating to Denmark. We see Witek kissing Czuszka; Witek making love to Olga; Witek crying uncontrollably at the station after his father dies and Witek asking the dean of the medical school for a sabbatical. The final image is Witek buying a student ticket and running for the train. As he runs through the station, he knocks into an older woman who drops some change, one coin of which rolls to the foot of a tramp who picks it up and buys a beer. Just like the coin that Karol in *Three Colours: White* cannot get rid of, this coin symbolises fate – and the crucial turning point in Witek's life.

Recurring Images: Mirrors. One of the twelve opening images sees a young Witek being taught maths by his father. He is viewed initially via his reflection, but then the camera swings round and we see the scene objectively. In Werner's flat, Witek goes to the bathroom, and is seen reflected in the mirror.

The gift of life. When Witek visits the woman whose home has been ransacked by government thugs, she tells him: "Life is a gift," something that Pawel's aunt will tell him in *Decalogue 1*. Similarly, when Witek speaks to God, he tells him "I am here," an echo of the computer that reads "I am ready" in *Decalogue 1*. Finally, when Witek's Jewish girlfriend leaves on a train, the couple press their hands together on each side of the train window - an image repeated in *Three Colours: Red*.

Verdict: Kieslowski's most well-known work before *The Decalogue*, but the director's criticisms hit the mark: an interesting idea, but too mechanically executed. 2/5

No End (Bez Konca, 1984)

Cast: Grzyna Szapolowska (Urszula), Jerzy Radziwillowicz (Antek), Maria Pakulnis (Joanna), Aleksander Bardini (Labrador), Artur Barcis (Darek)

Crew: Direction Krzysztof Kieslowski, Screenplay Krzysztof Kieslowski & Krzysztof Piesiewicz, Cinematography Jacek Petrycki, Music Zbigniew Preisner, Feature film, 107 minutes

Story: Antek, a lawyer, died of a heart attack a few days before *No End* opens. In the opening scene, his ghost watches over his sleeping widow Urszula who wakes, and is unaware of his presence. When alive, Antek worked as a lawyer; the case he was working on when he died was that of Darek, a young man who started a strike in a factory. Darek's wife Joanna calls Urszula to ask her for the files of the case; when Urszula rebuffs her, Joanna comes to Urszula's flat and begs her to help find a replacement lawyer. Urszula recommends Antek's former professor, Labrador, who is reluctant to take the case because he will soon be forced to take early retirement, but eventually agrees. After Urszula has dropped her son off to school and is on the way to Joanna's, her car mysteriously cuts out. Another car, hooting loudly, overtakes her. When her car just as mysteriously restarts, Urszula finds the overtaking car has crashed into a bus and its occupants killed. Meanwhile, as the legal case against Darek progresses it emerges that Darek's aims are not the same as his new lawyer's. Labrador wants to free Darek, while the accused is concerned with his principals and goes on hunger strike in protest. Urszula deals with her increasingly painful loss. She loves her son, but only now realises how much she loved Antek, and how much she misses him. She even tries hypnotherapy, but instead of helping her to forget, the session results in Urszula seeing Antek clearly before her. After an old friend of Antek's confesses to Urszula that the two men always fell for the same women, Urszula picks up an English tourist who thinks she is a prostitute. Again, she feels a strong connection with Antek. The court case closes and Darek gets an eighteen-month sentence but, as it is suspended for two years, he is free to leave. Finally, after dropping her son at his grandmother's house, Urszula methodically seals all air vents in the flat, turns on the gas cooker and kills herself. The last shot sees her joining Antek and they walk off into the dark together.

Background: In 1981, martial law was enforced by the Communist authorities in an attempt to crush the country's growing Solidarity movement. The atmosphere in Poland quickly became one of extreme intimidation, with courts passing long sentences for trivial misdemeanours; possession of an underground newspaper or writing graffiti on a wall were crimes punishable with long jail sentences. Kieslowski decided that he wanted to film some of these trials and met a young lawyer, Krzysztof Piesiewicz, who agreed to collaborate with him on exposing the judicial system. Lawyer and film-maker soon discovered that, as long as Kieslowski's cameras were recording these trials, judges seemed reluctant to hand out such unjust sentences. Soon Kieslowski was setting up in as many courtrooms as possible, often without film in his cameras!

Nothing ever came of recording these trials, but Kieslowski did decide that he wanted to make a film about martial law, and appointed Piesiewicz as his co-writer. Their film was indeed about the effects of martial law, but not about the tanks or the riots that resulted. "I thought at the time - and still do - that martial law was really a defeat for everyone, that everyone lost, that during martial law we all bowed our heads," said Kieslowski. This was a film about that defeat.

No End was badly received. The authorities made sure that it was screened at inaccessible cinemas and that newspapers misprinted screening times. The church objected to the sex and suicide scenes. And the political opposition didn't like it because Kieslowski hadn't shown them victorious at the end. Never again would Kieslowski use a political context for any of his films.

Comment: But even before he had a chance to become disillusioned by the film's reception, *No End* marked a new beginning for Kieslowski. In *Blind Chance* the director had explored the hypothetical; *No End* was the first film in which he took on the metaphysical, simultaneously a meditation on love, a political drama and a ghost story. Here we have an interventionist ghost who leaves his mark (literally, by putting a question mark

35

by Labrador's name on the list of lawyers, or in saving his wife's life by making her car engine cut out when she is on course for collision with a bus) and appears several times, watching over his nearest and dearest (when his son goes to school, when Urszula visits a hypnotherapist and again when she is unfaithful to him; Antek also appears when his former client is asleep in his cell and seems to spirit away a paper that Labrador wants to use to strike a compromise deal).

No End was also the start of two seminal relationships for Kieslowski: with writer Piesiewicz and composer Zbigniew Preisner, both of whom would go on to collaborate with Kieslowski on all his subsequent work.

Images: Candles. During martial law, a tradition evolved of leaving candles on window sills on the 13th of every month, through which people expressed communal anger at the political situation. In the opening scene, the candles in the cemetery represent death and allude to the later scene when Urszula and her son visit Antek's grave, but they also evoke this tradition to Polish audiences at the time.

Recurring Images: Hands. The first shot following the opening credits is of Antek's hand, which we then see gently touching the back of his sleeping son's head. Hands, with interlaced fingers or encircled around glasses, feature constantly throughout: when Urszula is talking to Jacek at the breakfast table, she places her bowed head in her hands; or when Urszula is talking to Antek's friend Tomek; at the hypnotherapist's, where he runs his finger around the rim of a glass and where Urszula communicates with Antek by playing a 'copycat' game of holding up a number of fingers. Finally, Urszula sleeps with the British tourist because his hands remind her of her dead husband's.

Mirrors and glass. When we first catch sight of Antek, we do not see him, but his ghostly reflection in a glass door. He is later reflected in the glass at the hypnotherapist's. Meanwhile, Urszula looks at herself in a mirror moments before she is unfaithful to Antek. Later she breaks down in tears by the bathroom mirror after she discovers her son listening to an opposition song.

And Another Thing: Lots of footage was shot with Jerzy Radziwillowicz (Antek), but very little made the final cut. No matter - at least for Polish audiences of the time. Radziwillowicz was chosen because his previous roles in Andrzej Wajda's films about the Solidarity movement, *Man Of Marble* and *Man Of Iron*, had made him known to the public as someone honourable. Kieslowski said: "I realised I had to hire him simply so that it would be clear to the audience that this man is someone who is inwardly extremely clean." And so Urszula's ultimate fidelity to her husband represents a fidelity to Solidarity.

Music: The musical refrain heard during the opening scene of *No End* and throughout was used as the basic refrain in *Three Colours: Blue*.

Verdict: Politics get in the way. Otherwise an entrancingly melancholic spectral love story. 3/5

The Decalogue (Dekalog, 1988)

Regular Cast: Artur Barcis (Young Man, aka The Witness)

Regular Crew: Direction Krzysztof Kieslowski, Screenplay Krzysztof Kieslowski & Krzysztof Piesiewicz, Music Zbigniew Preisner, Ten TV stories of approximately 55 minutes each

Although made as a ten-part series for Polish television in the late 1980s, *The Decalogue* is an extraordinary cinematic achievement. It debuted to great acclaim at the Venice Film Festival in 1989, thrusting Kieslowski into the international spotlight. Today, heavily-attended theatrical runs in Paris, New York or London (the four-hour instalments I attended, on rainy midweek evenings in west London, were sold out) keep him there. In their scope, wit, power and intelligence, there is nothing else quite like them.

Kieslowski was working at the Tor Film Studios under Krzysztof Zanussi when Piesiewicz, his co-writer on *No End*, suggested that someone should make a film about the Ten Commandments. And that someone should be Kieslowski. His phlegmatic response? "A terrible idea, of course." But one of the functions of the Tor Studios was to help young directors make their first film and Kieslowski thought that, with some funding from Polish television, a series of ten film scripts could be allocated to different directors which could then be presented on TV as a 'cycle' of instalments.

After initial research, Kieslowski and Piesiewicz settled down to write the screenplay. They decided they wanted to keep it secular - but not overbearingly so. "Everyday life was unbearably monotonous and terribly uninteresting," said the director. "We knew then that we had to find extreme, extraordinary situations for our characters, ones in which they would face difficult choices and make decisions which could not be taken lightly." But the hardships of Poland under Communism still emerge in *The Decalogue*: inhabitants have to boil water to take a bath, hospital ceilings leak, phone connections fail. Even the highrise flats bear the unmistakable concrete facade of totalitarian rule. "It's the most beautiful housing estate in Warsaw," said

Kieslowski. "It looks pretty awful, so you can imagine what the other are like."

Kieslowski finally settled on the high-rise setting (which also suited his camera's love of windows, mirrors and reflections) after rejecting several other methods of electing a character, or story, by chance - picking out a face from a huge stadium or following one person out of a crowded street. Here, behind every window lives a human being, another life worth scrutinising. In the opening instalment, the illusion of having plucked one of those lives at random is created by a pigeon from a startled flock that just happens to alight on Pawel's window ledge, and looks through the window into the flat.

But even after more than a year's work on the screenplay, something was still missing. Kieslowski discussed it for hours with Piesiewicz and with his literary agent, Witek Zaleski. One day Zaleski told the other two an anecdote about an author who, on seeing a film, commented to the director that he liked it very much, noting the cemetery scene and said he liked the guy in a black suit. When the director denied that there was any such figure, the author protested. He had seen him, on the left-hand side of the frame, then he had walked across to the right-hand side of the frame and moved off. The author was adamant that not only had he seen him, but that that particular moment was the best bit of the film. Ten days later the writer was dead. When Kieslowski heard this anecdote, he understood what was missing from the screenplay. It was "this guy in a black suit whom not everyone sees and who the young director didn't know had appeared in the film. But some people saw him, this guy who looks on. He doesn't have any influence on what's happening, but he is a sort of sign or warning to those whom he watches, if they notice him...So I introduced the character whom some called 'the angel.'" In the screenplay he was called the Young Man. I call him The Witness.

It took Kieslowski and Piesiewicz more than a year to co-write the scripts. By the end of it, Kieslowski had become attached to some of the stories and "rather selfishly" decided he wanted to direct all ten. What he did instead was hire a different cinematographer for each film, and spend the next 21 months filming and editing. He would occasionally shoot part of one film in the morning, part of a second at another location in the afternoon, and a third one in the evening.

Kieslowski intended for each instalment of *The Decalogue*, although based on the Ten Commandments, to remain untitled. While the cycle was designed to be approached with its theme - the Commandments - known from the outset, these were not spelt out in the titles. The relationship between the films and the individual Commandments was to be a tentative one: the films and their Commandments are often interchangeable, or the films pertain to more than one Commandment. Kieslowski hoped the audience would be stimulated into debating them.

But baffled critics insisted on knowing which film went with which Commandment and Kieslowski was forced to reduce the films to a list, which is used below. *Decalogue 1*, for instance, was titled: *I am the Lord thy God. Thou shalt have no other God but Me* (the First Commandment), but could just as easily relate to the Second Commandment (Thou shalt not make to thyself any graven image) and the Third Commandment (Thou shalt not take the name of the Lord thy God in vain). Similarly *2* is linked with the Third Commandment, but also relates to the Sixth Commandment (Thou shalt not kill), the Seventh (Thou shalt not commit adultery) and the Ninth (Thou shalt not bear false witness against thy neighbour). And so on. In his introduction to the English edition of the screenplay, Kieslowski wrote: "We endeavoured to construct the plot of this film so that the viewer would leave the film with the same questions in mind which we had asked ourselves when the screenplay was only an empty page fed into the typewriter." They were not designed to be read as strict moral codas, but rather as fodder for discussion; a starting point rather than a final statement.

Decalogue 1

Cast: Henry Karanowski (Krzysztof), Wojciech Klata (Pawel), Maja Komorowska (Irena)

Crew: Cinematography Wieslaw Zdort, 53 minutes

Commandment: I Am The Lord Thy God. Thou Shalt Have No Other God But Me

Story: Eleven-year-old Pawel is the brilliant son of Krzysztof, a professor who believes in logic and science. Together they delight in solving mathematical conundrums on their computers. After seeing a dead dog, Pawel's curiosity is aroused about death and the soul. Placing his faith in science, the professor explains simply that death occurs when the body ceases to function but denies the existence of the soul. Later Krzysztof's sister Irena, a devout Catholic, tries to share her faith with Pawel. When the boy asks about God, she hugs him and explains that God is in the love of their embrace. When the pond outside the high-rise where Pawel and Krzysztof live freezes over, Pawel admits that he has discovered his Christmas gift - a pair of skates - in a closet, and asks if he might have them early to skate on the pond. Father and son happily calculate that the thickness of the ice on the local pond would hold someone three times Pawel's weight. But when Pawel fails to return the next day after school, Krzysztof realises that the sirens and crowd by the lake can mean only one thing. After his son's body is pulled out of the water, Krzysztof goes to church and despairingly pushes the altar over: a candle drips onto a picture of the virgin Mary and gives the impression that she is weeping.

Comment: This first instalment of *The Decalogue* sets out the serious and thoughtful tone of the entire work. Dramatising the conflict between the spiritual and the rational, *1* tackles one of the most traumatic and incomprehensible scenarios - the death of a child - a theme which reoccurs in *2*, *5* and again in *8*. Underlining the fatalistic theme from the outset, one of the first images is that of Pawel frozen on the TV screen (just as he is frozen under the ice), a child whose fate is already sealed. There can be no going back. Kieslowski follows with a rigorously unsentimental and thought-provoking chapter.

41

There are no answers here, just questions. Why does Pawel die? Why does the ice break? Why does the ink spill? How does the computer switch itself on? What is it ready for? Finally, Pawel's own question: What remains after death? The father's unknowing response is that it is the memory of a person that remains: that they were kind, that they had a tooth missing, their smile. Poignantly, it is Pawel's joyful face captured on film by the camera crew at his school that remains for us and for his aunt Irena, who sees it after his death.

Kieslowski offers us no rational explanation for the breaking of the ice. In the screenplay, Kieslowski and Piesiewicz had an electricity generator release warm water into the lake without warning, but this was edited out whilst filming. Instead, the final version suggests divine interference, punishment for an excessive faith in technology. Pawel's rationalist father lectures in his class that one day computers will have aesthetic preferences, a personality even. Pawel can program his computer to lock and unlock doors, to turn taps on and off. He can even program it to tell him what his absent mother is doing at any given time of day. But it cannot tell him what she dreams of - the realms of the subconscious and the metaphysical are beyond the reach of even this computer. Computers cannot provide us with the definitive answer but, like the chess that Pawel plays so avidly, they teach us that there are always several options open to us. Choosing the right one is the hard part - and also the ethical dilemma outlined in 2.

The Witness: Decalogue 1 also introduces the wordless Witness, and he appears here more often and more prominently than in any other film of the series. The film opens with a desolate shot of the frozen lake. The only life form here is a young man, seated beside a smoking fire, who looks confrontationally into the camera. He is seen several more times in *1*: when Irena sheds a tear on seeing Pawel on the television screen, the film cuts to The Witness also wiping away a tear (although as always with Kieslowski, nothing is clear cut - he may be empathising with Irena, he may merely have soot in his eye); he is also shown following a shot of the church; after Irena defines God to Pawel; following the scene of the boy visiting his father's lecture; and finally when Krzysztof goes out at night to check if the ice will hold Pawel's weight. Later, when the police search for bodies under the broken ice Krzysztof notices the young man's fire, but it has burnt out and The Witness is conspicuously absent.

Images: Liquid out of control. The ice of the frozen lake opens the film while the last shot is of Pawel, frozen on a TV screen, just as he has been frozen under the ice on the lake. The ink that inexplicably stains Krzysztof's paper is a warning for him that liquid is out of control. Meanwhile milk, the drink of the young and symbolic of Pawel's absent mother, either turns sour or freezes. Even the holy water (which Krzysztof holds up to his forehead in the church) is frozen.

Look Out For: The Witness. He'll be cropping up in various guises throughout the ten-film series.

Verdict: An awesome, unforgettable introduction. 5/5

Decalogue 2

Cast: Krystyna Janda (Dorota), Aleksander Bardini (Doctor), Olgerd Lukaszewicz (Andrzej)

Crew: Cinematography Edward Klosinski, 57 minutes

Commandment: Thou Shalt Not Take The Name Of The Lord Thy God In Vain

Story: An irascible and elderly doctor is approached by a neighbour of his, Dorota. She explains that her husband Andrzej is seriously ill in the local hospital, on the doctor's ward, and she needs to know whether he is going to live or die. The physician brusquely tells her to see him during visitors' hours at the hospital. When she does, he still cannot give her an answer and he evades her when she persists in her demands back at the apartment block. She finally explains that she needs to know because, after seeming infertile, she is three months pregnant with her lover's child. Even though this could be her last chance of motherhood she will have an abortion if her husband is to recover. As the doctor still desists in giving her a prognosis, she books herself in for an abortion. But the doctor, whose own young family was killed in the war, calls her and tells her that

43

Andrzej is going to die. Miraculously though, Dorota's husband recovers - and is delighted by the news of her pregnancy.

Comment: If the first instalment of *The Decalogue* sets out the serious and thoughtful tone of the work, the second focuses on its moral complexity. An irascible doctor swears to Dorota under oath that her husband will die so that she cancels her abortion. Having seen slides suggesting Andrzej's miraculous recovery is already on its way, the doctor has taken the name of the Lord in vain. But he makes his decision in favour of life which, as Pawel's aunt Irena told him (and us) in *1*, is a gift. Dorota's unborn child gets to live, as does her husband, and the doctor has saved two lives instead of one. The reiteration of this story in *8* - as a scenario outlined in an ethics class - shows that nothing has become any easier during the course of *The Decalogue*, and that true dilemmas never really go away.

With the action focusing on the inner, ethical struggle, Kieslowski's emphasis in *2* is on close-ups, achieving a realism rarely seen on screen: clothes, hair and faces are as real as the dilemma. But Kieslowski's stringent realism never excludes allegoric imagery, and in *2* the director allows himself two eloquent scenes. In the first, Dorota peers down through her flat's blinds as the doctor walks past. Music underlines the scene's significance as she begins to pluck leaves from a plant, one by one. Finally she twists the stalk but is unable to snap it. Upon release, its elasticity allows a mesmerisingly slow recoil, suggesting a life force that refuses to be broken. The second moment begins as a stylistic tour de force, ending in an even more obvious allegory than that of the plant. Again, Dorota looks out of her window, this time straight ahead into the camera. The camera slides downwards and we see the doctor, also looking out of his window. It then swooshes to arrive at Andrzej's hospital bed, where he is looking much improved. Panning across, the camera finally comes to rest on a wasp painfully struggling to pull itself out of the remains of a jar of fruit compote that Dorota brought earlier. Hoisting itself up by the spoon, the wasp eventually frees itself from the unctuous liquid; it has, of course, also enacted Andrzej's escape from certain death, just as the plant earlier suggested his will to live.

For the final scene, when Dorota's husband tells the doctor his joy at the news of his wife's pregnancy, Kieslowski added two lines that are not in the published screenplay: "Do you understand what it means to have a child?" Andrzej asks the doctor. The mournful reply is, "I do." We see connections to both the doctor's own life and *1*. On two occasions, over a coffee with his cleaning lady, the doctor has spoken of the joy he had from his young family - all killed by a bomb in the war. In response to Andrzej's question, the doctor not only understands the joy but also, like Krzysztof from *1*, the agonising sorrow that having children can bring.

Images: Yet more liquid, which is here the symbol for life. At first though, as in *1*, it seems to signify death: drips from the leaking ceiling in the hospital fall into a bloody bedpan. But these drips also mark the passage of time and, with it, Andrzej's recovery.

The Witness: He makes two appearances here: he is first seen when slides reveal the progression of Andrzej's illness; and he is in the background of Andrzej's room when Dorota tells him she loves him. Both moments could be interpreted as turning points in the patient's return to life.

Look Out For: No characters intersect with this story, although both the doctor and Dorota and her husband appear in later ones: the doctor in *4* and Dorota and Andrzej in *5*. The moral dilemma faced by the doctor - in deciding whether he can give a prognosis on Dorota's husband thus also making a decision on the unborn child's life, is set as a scenario in an ethics class in *8*.

Verdict: Rigorously moral and ethical dilemma set within Kieslowski's humanist frame. 4/5

Decalogue 3

Cast: Daniel Olbrychski (Janusz), Maria Pakulinis (Eva)

Crew: Cinematography Piotr Sobocinski, 56 minutes

Commandment: Honour The Sabbath Day

Story: It is Christmas Eve. Janusz comes home with presents for his wife and children dressed as Santa Claus. Later he takes his family to Midnight Mass where he sees his former lover, Eva. Back at home the doorbell rings and Janusz excuses himself abruptly, telling his wife that someone has stolen his taxi. Outside he is met by Eva who tells him that her husband, Edward, has disappeared. Janusz reluctantly spends the night driving around with Eva, visiting the hospital morgue and a centre for alcoholics - where sleeping drunks are callously hosed down with freezing water - in a fruitless search for Edward. Eventually they end up at the train station where Eva sees the clock turn 7: 03 a.m. Eva reveals that, at this precise time three years ago, Edward left her after finding her in bed with Janusz. She confesses that she has used Janusz as part of a superstitious scheme to change her luck, making a bet with herself: if she could get Janusz to spend the night with her, in any way, she would not kill herself. Janusz returns to his wife, who suspects he was with Eva all along.

Comment: Those with a keen eye and memory will notice Krzysztof from *1* making an early appearance here. He bumps into Janusz who, dressed as Santa Claus, is on his way to deliver presents to his children. Kieslowski both alludes to Krzysztof's earlier tragedy (he will not be dressing up as Santa this year, or any other) but also sets the sad theme for this instalment: not everyone celebrates at Christmas. The camera pans from Krzysztof's haunted face through Janusz's first floor window and we see a happy family watched by a man who has lost his own. Who wouldn't feel desperate in such a position? It is the suicidal moods that dog the isolated at times such as these that is the premise behind this oppressive and claustrophobic nocturnal outing.

But while Kieslowski clearly sets up to his themes from the outset, we are left to discover the specific reasons behind Eva's summoning of Janusz from the bosom of his family. The idea of death is first invoked by a razor that Eva hastily plants as evidence of Edward's existence in her life, when she finally lures Janusz back to her apartment. But the notion of suicide is thwarted when we see that the razor is blunt; it draws no blood when first Janusz and then Eva test it against themselves. It's only when Eva finally suggests the notion herself with the pill that she pulls from her pocket, that her previously bizarre behaviour - planting the razor blade, the elaborate lie that takes them to the centre for alcoholics in search of Edward - is explained. Having shared Janusz's ignorance of the true state of affairs, once it is revealed we, like him, are forced to modify our attitude towards Eva from one of exasperation to compassion. But it seems that compassion is in short supply in Warsaw on this holiest of nights. "It's difficult to be alone on a night like this," Eva tries to explain and Janusz finishes her sentence: "People shut themselves in and draw the curtains." And then he goes home to his wife.

Images: Kieslowski employs expressive camera work in *3*, focusing on light and glass in particular. From the opening shot, of blurred lights which slowly come into focus, to the police lights and the headlights of their cars as Janusz and Eva say goodbye to each other, there is little natural light in this nocturnal film. Especially striking is the lighting at the station when only Janusz's and Eva's eyes are illuminated, indicating a new honesty between them (an idea which is repeated in *9* when Roman and Hanka are in the lift). The presence of glass and mirrors conveys separation and deceit.

Recurring Themes: Colours. The red, white & blue of clothes and the police cars pre-empts the later *Three Colours Trilogy*.

The Witness: He appears on the approaching tram in the tunnel, which Janusz and Eva skid to avoid.

Look Out For: Krzysztof from *1*, who passes Janusz when he is on his way home dressed as Santa Claus.

Verdict: Laboriously contrived and plotted, this is less an illumination of Eva's motivation than a lengthy expose of her situation. 3/5

Decalogue 4

Cast: Adrianna Biedrzynska (Anka), Janusz Gajos (Michal)

Crew: Cinematography Krzysztof Pakulski, 55minutes

Commandment: Honour Thy Father And Thy Mother

Story: It is Easter. Anka, a 20-year-old drama student, lives with her widowed father Michal with whom she has an uninhibited and spontaneous relationship. Intrigued by an envelope discovered hidden in a drawer labelled "To be opened only after my death", she opens it while he is away. It contains a sealed letter to Anka written by her mother. Upon her father's return, Anka tells him that she has read the letter and learned that he is not her biological father. She also admits that that knowledge has also liberated her sexual feelings towards Michal, who she has always thought of when making love to any boyfriend. Although Michal acknowledges his own, troubled feelings towards Anka, he refuses to act upon them and rejects her advance. Upset, Anka falls asleep. On waking, she discovers Michal gone. Running after him, she confesses that she didn't read the letter after all, and made up its contents. Together, they burn the letter, the remains of which hint that Anka's guess was correct.

Comment: Continuing the parent/child theme of *1* and *2*, in *4* Kieslowski tackles the most troubling scenario: incest. It's also a situation that could hypothetically be the future outcome of *2*, in which a man embraces a child that is not biologically his.

Kieslowski also returns to a religious context. While *3* takes place on Christmas Eve, *4* is set during Easter, an event during which customs allow for the opening scene of a man and a woman (we do not yet know their relationship) throwing water over each other. Having introduced themes carefully in the first three instalments, Kieslowski is now confident to quickly show that there's something amiss here. It is immediately clear that their intimacy is not that of a father and his daughter, and we are left wondering about the exact nature of their relationship until Anka finally addresses Michal as "dad" when she receives a phone call. But what father (even given the excuse of an Easter custom?) would throw a bucket of water over his daughter when she is wearing nothing but a flimsy cotton nightdress? What daughter would protest, but really laugh and relish the joke?

As a drama student, Anka learns the art of performance. She pretends to have discovered that Michal is not her father, and perhaps she and Michal have merely been acting out their father and daughter roles all this time? Notably, in her acting class she is only convincing in the role of lover when her teacher, a man of her father's generation, plays opposite her. When she acts out the role of seductress with Michal, however, he rejects her. In an ironic twist on the commandment that *4* relates to ("Honour thy father and thy mother") Anka discovers that the only true way to honour her father is by disobeying her mother and decides to burn the letter. The pair must now return to some semblance of normality, acting out their roles of father and daughter.

Images: Spectacles and sight. Anka goes to the optician who asks her to spell out the word 'FATHER' while testing her vision, before providing her with a ridiculous pair of frames. At the outset of the tale, Anka cannot see clearly. By the end, both she and her father have gained some clarity. This image, combined with its theme of incest, clearly invokes the tale of Oedipus. But instead of an unwitting child sleeping with its parent, here a child deliberately destroys the parental bond in order to pave the way for a sexual relationship. Oedipus slept with his mother and plucked out his eyes because of it; Anka doesn't sleep with Michal, and is allowed to keep her glasses.

The Witness: He can be seen rowing on the lake when Anka is examining the letter, walking past with the canoe hoisted on his shoulders. The gaze he directs at Anka perhaps prevents her from opening the letter. Later, he walks past when Anka tells Michal that she lied about reading the letter.

Look Out For: The doctor from *2*, who walks in on father and daughter when they are in the lift.

Verdict: A contemporary interpretation of the Greek myth of Oedipus. Intriguing and perfectly paced. 4/5

Decalogue 5

Cast: Miroslaw Baka (Jacek), Krzysztof Globisz (Piotr), Jan Tesarz (Taxi Driver), Zbigniew Zapasiewicz (Law School Examiner)

Crew: Cinematography Slawomir Idziak, 57 minutes

Commandment: Thou Shalt Not Kill

Story: A disaffected twenty-year-old, Jacek, seems to wander through life immersed in its brutality - he drops rocks off a bridge to smash car windscreens below and knocks over a man in an urinal for no apparent reason. He also goes to a photographer's to have a picture of a young girl enlarged and stops off at a café where he has a joke with two passing young girls. Leaving, Jacek takes a taxi, instructs the driver to take a deserted road and without warning places a rope that he has been toying with all day around the driver's neck. This throttling is not enough to kill the struggling driver, so Jacek beats him, pulls him out of the car and bashes his head in with a rock. An idealistic young lawyer who is against capital punishment, Piotr, is called in to defend Jacek, but fails and the death sentence is handed out. Preparations for the final scene include the checking of the execution equipment (a hanging chamber) and a last conversation between Piotr and Jacek, who tells the lawyer a story of how his 12-year-old sister (the girl in the photo) was killed by a tractor. Guards come for Jacek and, in a scene as brutal as the one in which Jacek killed the taxi driver, he is executed. Piotr drives to the country in his car and shouts: "I abhor it," over and over again.

Comment: Kieslowski's fifth Decalogue instalment stands out from the others in that it advocates a commandment - Thou shalt not kill - rather than merely posing a dilemma. This instalment essentially argues the senseless cruelty of both a crime and its punishment. It starts with Piotr, the young lawyer, outlining his argument on freedom, responsibility and the fallacy of deterrent sentencing for criminals and ends with him repeatedly screaming "I abhor it."

Shocking, nauseating, raw and emotive, 5 is an extremely difficult viewing experience, even in this shorter version

(Kieslowski went on to make this and the following Decalogue into feature-length films). Moving away from the domestic terrain of *The Decalogue 1-4*, *5* also takes us physically away from the housing complex and disorientates us by taking us into unfamiliar territory. With the first four instalments Kieslowski offered us character motivation and encouraged sympathy for his protagonists (even the curt and dismissive doctor in *2*). In *5* there is a deliberate withholding of background information on both of the characters, and we know almost nothing about either Jacek or the taxi driver (we never find out the taxi driver's name and we only find out Jacek's when he is sentenced). We are not allowed to identify with either and forced to view events objectively. Filtered through an evil green light, Warsaw is presented as a desolate place, and the alienated Jacek seems completely removed from those around him. (He ignores a gang of youths beating someone up, scares away pigeons an old woman is feeding, and knocks over a man who smiles at him in the urinal).

While the feature-length *A Short Film About Killing* suggests a possible reason for Jacek's violent act (to steal the car), this is not referred to in *5*. Jacek's victim is chosen completely at random and the murderer is motiveless in his crime. Kieslowski's obsession with chance and fate once more takes centre stage here. The first hints come when Jacek lets the stone drop off the bridge, letting fate decide whether or not it smashes a car windscreen and causes an accident. But the pivotal moments begin to occur when the taxi driver plays a cruel trick on Dorota and her husband. What if he'd given them a lift instead? Or what if the other customers had got into the taxi before Jacek?

People take a long time to die. Even edited down to just under five minutes (in the feature-length version, the murder scene, at more than seven minutes, is one of the longest ever recorded on celluloid) the murder scene is gruesomely lengthy and realistic, while it takes the state a similar length of time to execute a struggling Jacek. Jacek's attitude to murder is mirrored by the impersonal way in which the state prepare for his execution. Finally, Piotr's despair in the car mirrors Jacek's outburst after he has managed to kill the taxi driver, throwing out the playing tape machine in disgust. Meanwhile, the audience is left with nothing but the green-hued tinge of nausea and despair.

Images: Mirror and glass. When he is introduced, Piotr is framed in a mirror. The driver first appears seen through a glass door in the apartment complex. Jack is reflected in the cinema window. There is more glass: at the movie theatre box office where Jacek speaks to the sales girl seated behind the partition; the café's window and glass tables; and in the windscreen of the taxi, which also has a rear-view and side mirrors. Glass is used to distance the audience, to help it retain its objectivity, to aid it to observe and judge. Mirrors meanwhile tell us that this is a story that reflects the cruelty of the world. They also allude to Kieslowski's mirroring of the two killings.

The Witness: First appearing in 5 just before the murder, The Witness looks into the taxi and shakes his head, as if to warn Jacek from carrying out his plan. He then seems to appear just before the execution scene, with a ladder. As this appearance also coincides with the judge congratulating Piotr on the birth of his son, it seems to indicate that The Witness simultaneously celebrates new life, while mirroring his first appearance in trying to prevent a killing.

Look Out For: Dorota and her husband, approaching the taxi driver for a ride.

Verdict: Highly effective and traumatic anti-violence argument. 5/5

Decalogue 6

Cast: Grazyna Szaplowski (Magda), Olaf Lubaszenko (Tomek), Stefania Iwinska (Landlady)

Crew: Cinematography Witold Adamek, 58 minutes

Commandment: Thou Shalt Not Commit Adultery

Story: Tomek, a timid and pale nineteen-year-old postal worker, is obsessed with Magda, an attractive artist in her thirties who lives across the courtyard from him. Every night, he sets his alarm clock for 8.30 to alert him of Magda's arrival home, whereupon he spies on her and her lovers through a stolen telescope. To get personal contact with her, he places forged money orders into her mailbox to draw her to the post office and even gets a job delivering milk on her round. After finally confessing his love to her, they go out on a date and end up at her apartment. There, Tomek confesses that he is a virgin and Magda leads his nervous hand up her thigh. After his quick climax she dismisses him harshly, telling him that that is all there is to love. Tomek runs home where he slits his wrists. Meanwhile Magda, unaware of Tomek's suicide attempt, is overcome with guilt at her insensitive behaviour. When she hears of his hospitalisation she tries to visit him, but is thwarted by Tomek's landlady, who witnessed the whole episode between them through Tomek's telescope. On Tomek's return to the post office, Magda is delighted to see him, but he merely tells her he no longer spies on her.

Comment: Having done his best to distance the viewer from the characters in 5, Kieslowski now does his best to implicate the audience in 6, drawing us vicariously into the action. Tomek is the central Peeping Tom, but Kieslowski extends the voyeurism to all the major characters and to the audience itself. The glass lens of the telescope alludes to the glass lens of Witold Adamek's camera - indeed, the first time we see Magda in her flat is through Tomek's telescope as he spies on her. Tomek himself has assumed the place of his friend Marcin, who bequeathed him not only his room, but his opera glasses. Later Tomek's place at the telescope (he upgrades his equipment through theft early on in the film) is in turn assumed by his landlady, Marcin's mother, so she can spy on events when he visits Magda's apartment. After their disastrous meeting, it is Magda who rummages around for her opera glasses and desperately tries to search out Tomek in the apartment block opposite (in vain, as he is in the bathroom with the razor blade).

Again, chance and fate become intertwined in the lead up to Tomek's suicide attempt. On leaving the café, Magda suggests that they run for their bus; if they catch it, they go back to her place, if not, they don't. Kieslowski's obsession with the theme almost matches Tomek's obsession with Magda!

But if you think that 5 is just a Hitchcockian exercise in voyeurism, think again. It's more than that. It's a love story, as

Zbigniew Preisner's score makes plain. From the plaintive solitary guitar that accompanies unrequited lover Tomek spying on the object of his affection (and turning away when Magda makes love with someone else, implying that his gaze is one of love rather than lust), to the fully-blown romanticism that accompanies their scene in the café, Preisner's score endows *5* with a haunted longing. Tomek's voyeurism is not presented as contemptible in any way; there is a shyness that coexists with obsessive romanticism in his gaze. When he sees Magda weeping, the gorgeous music that sweeps in tells us this is no ordinary peep-show.

But Kieslowski was not just a humanist, he was a pessimist too. The ending to *5* (as opposed to the more optimistic conclusion to *A Short Film About Love*, discussed later) ends in depressing stasis. Two characters, who could have reached out and touched each other, are instead scarred (Tomek literally) by the episode, and the glass partition in the post office will forever separate them. "The television ending (as opposed to the ending of *A Short Film About Love*) is far closer to the view I have of how things really are in life," Kieslowski said.

Images: Glass and milk. Glass is the central motif and symbol here; it separates and divides people, but also allows them to observe each other. Even during the opening credits, Magda is reflected in the glass at the post office, while the second shot shows the shattering of glass as Tomek steals the telescope (also symbolising Tomek's attempts to break through and get closer to Magda). The glass lens of the telescope is also recalled by the glass lens of Kieslowski's camera, through which we, along with Tomek, observe Magda. Milk meanwhile symbolises maternal fluid; Magda is an older woman and Tomek, an orphan, was denied maternal love as a child. He becomes a milk delivery man in an attempt to get closer to Magda and milk is spilt both inside Magda's apartment and on her doorstep.

The Witness: When Magda agrees to go out with Tomek he can be seen smiling while watching Tomek excitedly pulling his milk trolley in a triumphant circle. But he is also there when Magda dismisses him, and a humiliated Tomek passes him as he rushes back home across the courtyard. The Witness is dressed in white, a reflection of Tomek's innocence.

Look Out For: The man wheeling a bicycle past Tomek as he puts the forged postal orders into Magda's letter box - he will appear again as Roman in 9.

Verdict: Haunting and elegiac story of unrequited love. 5/5

Decalogue 7

Cast: Anna Polony (Ewa), Maja Barelkowska (Majka), Wladyslaw Kowalski (Stefan), Katarzyna Piwowarczyk (Ania), Boguslaw Linda (Wojtek)

Crew: Cinematography Dariusz Kuc, 55 minutes

Commandment: Thou Shalt Not Steal

Story: Majka, a sullen young woman, kidnaps six-year-old Ania from a theatre and takes her by train to the countryside. Ania is known as Majka's much younger sister, but it soon emerges that she is in fact her daughter - the result of a liaison between a teenage Majka and one of the teachers at school, where her mother was the headmistress. To avoid scandal, Majka's mother, Ewa, raised Ania as her own. Majka takes Ania to see Wojtek, the girl's biological father, who now makes teddy bears for a living. He reluctantly lets them stay. While they talk, Majka confesses to him that she once saw her mother breast-feeding Ania. Later, a distraught Ewa and Majka's father, Stefan, are stunned to receive a call from Majka demanding her rights of motherhood. They in turn call upon Wojtek to help them retrieve Ania, who has been taken by Majka to the local train station. Upon discovery, Ania welcomes the older woman as her mother and an upset Majka jumps onto a departing train, chased by Ania to the end of the platform.

Comment: If the closing image of 5 - that of Magda behind a glass partition - is one of isolation, then this is repeated in one of the opening shots of 6. The image of Majka behind the glass window of the passport office is paralleled with the shot of her face framed behind the train window at the end. Nothing has changed for her and she leaves on the train perhaps even lonelier than when we were first introduced to her. (Notably, as in

Blind Chance, the catching of a train does not suggest escape or freedom, but the fulfilment of a destiny).

Images of loneliness are plentiful. We see Majka spying on Ania from the shrubbery, separated from her by a fence, literally barred from her own daughter. Following the kidnapping, Ania's ride on a deserted merry-go-round invokes a lost childhood, rather like the hundreds of teddy bears that Wojtek, the absent father, now makes a living from. Stacked up against each other, their sheer numbers, and the lack of any children to play with them, are an eloquent symbol.

A web of deceit and theft is woven into the tapestry of *7*. Majka tells her mother that she stole her daughter from her, but perhaps Ewa was over-eager to do so because she was 'robbed' of the chance of more children after having Majka. Wojtek stole Majka's childhood, but Ewa and Majka 'robbed' him of the chance to be a father. The verbal reference to a commandment here, when Majka asks: "Can you steal something that's yours?" is too explicit, too clumsy. Kieslowski hammers home the point, and the reference to a specific commandment seems too direct.

Images: Hands. The first close-up of a hand is the one on Majka's shoulder as she tries to comfort he screaming Ania. But instead of providing comfort, the hand turns out to belong to Ewa, and pushes Majka away. Later on we see Majka introducing Ania to Wojtek, with her hands clasped around her daughter's neck, and when the young girl falls asleep surrounded by teddy bears, she clasps hold of Wojtek's finger, suggesting the unconscious strength of the biological bond. Kieslowski's liking for a red-white-blue colour scheme is once again employed, with Ania dressed in a white blouse with a red coat, Wojtek's red phone and van set against the shots of tranquil blue water during the search for Ania.

The Witness: In the screenplay, The Witness appears in the last scene as a man on crutches on the platform who gets off the train and looks over towards the waiting room. After shooting the scene however, Kieslowski decided that close-up footage of The Witness was unusable, although he can be seen in the background getting off the train as Majka jumps on. The Witness also appears in the screenplay - later deleted from the film - during a conversation between Majka and Ania just as the girl sets off for the theatre.

Look Out For: No one from any other instalment appears in 7, although Ania makes a brief appearance in 9.

Verdict: Perhaps because this episode follows the two most affecting segments that were worthy of feature-length treatment, 7 is one of the least satisfactory segments in *The Decalogue*. The self-critical Kieslowski deemed it too wordy in its exposition of events leading up to the kidnapping. An affecting performance by Maja Barelkowska as the sullen/petulant/cunning terrorist sister/mother fails to lift it. 2/5

Decalogue 8

Cast: Maria Koscialkowska (Zofia), Teresa Marczewska (Elisabeth), Tadeusz Lomnicki (Tailor)

Crew: Cinematography Andrzej Jaroszewicz, 55 minutes

Commandment: Thou Shalt Not Bear False Witness

Story: Zofia is a respected professor of philosophy. One day the Dean of her university introduces her to Elisabeth Lorenc, a young philosopher from New York who has translated Zofia's works and now wants to sit in on some of her classes. During a debate on 'ethical hell' Elisabeth tells a story that discomforts the professor... In 1943, a six-year-old Jewish girl was brought to hide with a couple in their Warsaw apartment. The woman who was supposed to protect the girl told her that they had to withdraw the offer because their religion forbids the bearing of false witness - which, in this case, would mean lying to the authorities. It becomes apparent that the two women have a personal, as well as a professional, connection and this story relates directly to them.

After the class Zofia expresses relief that Elisabeth survived. They then revisit the old apartment block where the exchange took place, and Elisabeth scares the old professor by hiding from her.

Back at Zofia's flat, Zofia explains that she withdrew the offer, and that Elisabeth's transfer to the next couple was blocked because they were rumoured to be linked to the Gestapo and might have betrayed the underground organisation to which Zofia and her husband belonged. Zofia adds that that information later turned out to be false and that the couple - a tailor and his wife - only narrowly escaped execution because of it. On Elisabeth's request, Zofia takes her to see the tailor, but he refuses to speak to her about his past.

Comment: Who, or what, is God? Certainly within a series based on the Ten Commandments this is the ultimate question. Who guides us? Who tells us what is right and wrong? What is faith? In *8*, Kieslowski presents us with the series' most blatantly philosophical instalment.

It is perhaps also the instalment that most closely espouses Kieslowski's own beliefs, and it is easy to interpret the character of Zofia, whose agnostic humanism is rooted in a spiritual belief, as Kieslowski's mouthpiece. When Zofia - whose name in Greek means wisdom - is questioned by Elisabeth about God, she replies: "I am reluctant to use the word 'God.' One can believe without having to use certain words. Man was created in order to choose...if so, perhaps we can leave God out of it."

But if we leave God out of it, what are we left with? "The world gives birth to Good or Evil," says Zofia. "That particular evening in 1943 did not bring out the Good in me." The evening when Zofia denied a six-year-old Elisabeth shelter is raised for discussion in the professor's class on ethical hell. Zofia's students are unaware that the protagonists of this particular moral dilemma are seated in front of them. But we guess their identities, and the look of The Witness implies that he knows too. Later, on visiting the old apartment where the women's first meeting took place, Elisabeth comments that "people don't like witnesses of their humiliation." Forty years ago it was Elisabeth who was humiliated, this time it has been Zofia, first in class and now during Elisabeth's vengeful game of hide-and-seek.

Revisiting the scene allows them to move on. At Zofia's apartment, the professor can finally fulfil the promise of shelter made more than forty years earlier. Elisabeth acknowledges the professor's moral courage and affectionately takes her hand in an image of trust that recalls the flashback that opened the instalment (a child's hand clasped in that of an adult's), and some kind of resolution is reached by both women.

But Kieslowski's decision to end with the scene with the tailor - the man who was due to shelter Elisabeth after Zofia, who was falsely accused of being linked with the Gestapo and nearly executed because of it - adds a poignancy to *8*. He is the true victim of the broken commandment, Thou shalt not bear false witness, and he cannot revisit his painful past. Watching the two women at the end of the film, he is excluded from their catharsis, a fact made symbolic by the window bars that separate him from Zofia and Elisabeth. The tailor is a reminder that, just like the picture in Zofia's apartment that refuses to be put straight, some things cannot be rectified so easily. As Zofia points out, "sometimes 'I'm sorry' is not enough."

Images: If hands are the central image to *7*, they are also integral to *8*. The opening image is that of a child's hand clasped in an adult's; it is only revealed to be a flashback much later. Next we see Zofia jogging in the park and, after she comes to rest during her press-ups, we see a close-up of her hands resting on a log. Elisabeth's fingers constantly play with the cross around her neck and she also places her hands around the cup of tea that is offered to her in Zofia's apartment replacing the one that she was denied many years ago. During the women's conversation in the professor's apartment, Zofia places her hands on Elisabeth's shoulders - and the younger woman reaches up to them with her own hands in a gesture of acceptance, forgiveness and trust.

The Witness: He appears in the classroom scene while Elisabeth recounts the tale of the Jewish child denied sanctuary. As she recounts her tale, the camera pans from her face to his, glancing directly into the camera, which is looking at him from where Zofia is seated behind her desk.

Look Out For: The neighbour who proudly shows Zofia his new stamps. His stamp collection is central to the plot of *10*. Also the story of *2* is outlined as a moral dilemma in Zofia's ethics class.

Verdict: Gruelling, intellectually challenging drama. 5/5

Decalogue 9

Cast: Ewa Blaszczyk (Hanka), Piotr Machalica (Roman), Jan Jankowski (Mariusz), Jolanta Pietek-Gorecka (Ola)

Crew: Cinematography Piotr Sobocinski, 58 minutes

Commandment: Thou Shalt Not Covet Thy Neighbour's Wife

Story: Roman, a highly respected surgeon, and his wife Hanka are very much in love. But when Roman learns that his impotence is incurable, he suggests a divorce. Devoted to her husband, Hanka refuses, saying that love is in the heart, not between the legs, and insists that they should focus on what they have rather than what they do not. Made suspicious by a phone call, Roman spies on his wife and discovers that she is having an affair with a student, Mariusz, holding secret trysts in her absent mother's apartment. Hanka ends her affair but is persuaded by her husband to go skiing in order to give the couple a break from each other. But on seeing Mariusz preparing to go to the mountains (the student has discovered where Hanka has gone and decided to follow her) Roman assumes that she has been lying to him all along and prepares to commit suicide. When Hanka sees Mariusz turn up at the ski resort she assumes the worst and, after desperately trying to call Roman, she rushes home to try and get to him in time. She reads his suicide note, but then gets a call from him in hospital - where he is encased in plaster from the neck down.

Comment: If *Decalogue 8* was linked to *Decalogue 2*, then *9* is an inverse reflection of *6*, and Roman's appearance in the earlier instalment can be no coincidence. Like *6*, we see a young man fall for an older woman, but this time, we see her side of the affair. Crucially though, unlike Magda, Hanka thinks that there is more to love than just sex: "Love is in one's heart, not between one's legs," she says. So why does she look away when Mariusz is making love to her?

The cross-cutting of shots between Hanka and Roman, their composition and the focus within them repeatedly suggest both separation and togetherness. Even when they are apart, this couple still seems as one. From the beginning Hanka can tell when something is wrong: at two crisis points in Roman's life, when he is told of his impotence and when he pushes his bike into the river, she awakes from her sleep with a start as if she were aware that something was wrong. But walls and doors constantly divide them or, if they are in the same frame, then often one is in focus in the foreground, the other in the background, unfocussed - or vice versa. They are apart even when they share the same lift. In a virtuoso set-up Kieslowski shows with the falling light - first spotlighting husband, then wife, then husband again - how they can be together and yet apart. The bathroom scene where Roman asks Hanka a physics question (having discovered Mariusz's exercise book in the car) is equally mesmerising. At first they seem to be looking in opposite directions, but as Hanka moves forward, her reflection reveals that she has been facing Roman all along. This mirror imaging also reflects Roman's predicament; his impotence makes him feel only half a man.

Philosophically, *9* asks the question: What do we need to live? Can Roman (and, by implication, Hanka) live without sex? Can Roman's patient live without singing? Although Roman and the patient (or at least her mother) seem to think the answer to this question is no, the answer perhaps lies in Hanka's response: "The things we have are more important than the things we do not have." Roman's miraculous escape from his suicide attempts (the appearance of The Witness implies that his near car crash after learning his impotence is incurable was also a suicide attempt) suggests a greater protective force at work. Echoing themes of chance or fate, Roman survives despite Hanka's frustrated long-distance calls to prevent him from going through with his plan and despite his own attempts. When they finally speak, her words, "God, you're there," can be read either as relief that Roman has survived or as acknowledgement of the divine powers that are smiling down on them.

Images: The omnipresent telephone. One telephone or another is often foregrounded in shots in *9*. From the opening scene when Hanka is waiting for a call from Roman to the closing scene which mirrors it, the phone is a dramatically charged object. Roman devises a bugging system to enable him to listen in on Hanka's calls, and then uses the phone to confirm his suspicions by calling Mariusz's number. In a panic, Hanka calls Roman from the ski resort, but her call is frustrated: firstly by a pushy local, then by the unreliable phone system and finally by Roman himself, already set on his course of action and refusing to answer the phone.

The Witness: Can be seen on two occasions. He is first seen cycling past when Roman nearly crashes his car after learning that his condition is incurable. The second time The Witness appears is when Roman is attempting suicide on his bike - Roman can be seen overtaking The Witness, who then appears in the background behind the turning spokes of Roman's stationary bicycle after he has deliberately cycled off the edge of the road.

Look Out For: The little girl Ania, from *7*, who makes an appearance playing in the courtyard as Roman looks out of his kitchen window. She can only be seen in the distance, but is identified in the script. She was also written into the opening scene of the screenplay, but this was not included in the final version. Also keep an eye out for an old woman who throws her rubbish in the skip after Roman has disposed of Mariusz's exercise book - the incident seems to have amused Kieslowski so much that he staged similar ones in his subsequent films.

And Another Thing: It was originally planned that *9* would be given the feature film treatment - to be expanded into *A Short Film About Jealousy* – but Kieslowski proved too tired for the task.

Verdict: This is the instalment that most obviously foreshadows Kieslowski's later work. The singer with a heart ailment and a predilection for Van den Budenmayer looks ahead to *The Double Life of Véronique*; while phone tapping, impotence and a blue colour scheme suggest the *Three Colours: Red, White* and *Blue* respectively. Brilliantly conceived and executed. 5/5

Decalogue 10

Cast: Jerzy Stuhr (Jerzy), Zbigniew Zamachowski (Artur), Henry Bista (Shopkeeper)

Crew: Cinematography Jacek Blawut, 57 minutes

Commandment: Thou Shalt Not Covet Thy Neighbour's Goods

Story: A reclusive stamp enthusiast (from 8) dies, leaving his collection to his two sons: Artur, a singer with punk band City Death, and the more conservative Jerzy. Ignorant of the collection's value, Jerzy gives three priceless Zeppelin stamps to his young son because he likes aeroplanes, but is horrified to later discover not only their value, but also that his son has exchanged them and they have ended up in the hands of a dishonest dealer. The brothers, increasingly obsessed by the collection, go to great lengths to protect the rest of it, including the acquisition of a black Doberman to keep guard - advice given by 'friends in the know' - and changing the locks on the apartment. Going through their father's notes, they discover that he coveted a rare Rose Mercury stamp. But no amount of money can purchase such a priceless thing. The dishonest dealer's daughter needs a kidney and Jerzy is a suitable donor. Artur talks his brother into having the operation. While Jerzy is in hospital and Artur busy with a star-struck nurse, the apartment is robbed and the brothers are left with nothing except the Austrian Rose Mercury. With the job bearing all the hallmarks of an inside job, each brother suspects the other until, having each purchased a new series of stamps, they spot the real culprits: the dealer, the youth who exchanged stamps with Jerzy's son, and a neighbour who claimed their father owed him money. All three own black Doberman dogs.

Comment: Just when you thought it was all getting too cerebral, Kieslowski lets rip. A black comedy of all things! The credit sequence establishes an ironic, upbeat vein with Artur, lead singer of punk rock band City Death, blasting out a song urging people to:

"Kill! Kill! Kill!

Commit adultery, covet things all the week.

And on Sunday, on Sunday,

Beating up your mother, your father, your sister,

Beat up the young and steal,

Because everything belongs to you.

Everything belongs to you."

The next scene shows Artur at his father's funeral, a man who sacrificed his life to a "noble passion." Artur's lugubrious brother Jerzy has to nudge him to turn his Walkman down. It is only later that we find out this noble passion was none other than collecting stamps.

Despite Artur's status as a rock star (and his lyrics) he initially appears free of covetousness. "Where does it come from, this urge to have something?" he asks his brother, when they first set eyes on their father's precious stamp collection. On discovering its true value however, (stamps apparently proving a more profitable pastime than being a rock star), he soon finds himself under its spell. It is Artur who installs the high-security arrangements, including acquiring the ludicrously large and menacing Doberman to stand guard. It is also Artur who becomes so obsessed with owning the Austrian Rose Mercury that he urges Jerzy to sacrifice a kidney in exchange for the priceless stamp, even using emotional blackmail in suggesting that he is morally obliged to help save the beneficiary - who also happens to be the dodgy dealer's daughter.

It is this covetousness that is the brothers' downfall. While Jerzy is having the operation and Artur having it away with the star-struck nurse, the kidney operation is cross-cut with another scene of something being removed: the stamp collection from the apartment. The stamp collection has reunited the brothers (before their father's death they had not seen each other for two years) and made them forget their problems. But the stamp collection also temporarily drives them apart when they suspect each other of the theft. When the brothers seem to have lost everything, with nothing left but the precious Austrian Rose Mercury, they finally discover they have something even more valuable than that: a new-found trust in each other. And brotherhood is what *10* - and all of *The Decalogue* for that matter - is really about. A Warsaw apartment block that is a microcosm for the dilemmas of mankind.

Images: Brotherhood. Jerzy and Artur are not just physically dissimilar, they are also at opposite ends of the spectrum, with Jerzy a bourgeois, married suit-and-tie man and Artur the bohemian rock star with a string of girls. Between these two characters lies the entire human race. But the stamp collection brings them together and they are often framed in the same shot: at the funeral, going into their father's apartment for the first time, outside at night when checking the apartment for security.

Keys. There are several shots of keys in this instalment, particularly at the beginning when the brothers first enter the apartment; Artur later changes the locks. Perhaps Kieslowski is suggesting that *10* - with its theme of brotherhood - is the key to the rest of *The Decalogue*.

The Witness: He was never written into the screenplay for this one. Later Kieslowski said: "He doesn't appear in film *10* because, since there are jokes about trading a kidney, I thought that maybe it's not worth showing a guy like that. But I was probably wrong. No doubt I should have shown him in that one, too."

Look Out For: Tomek, from *6*, still in his post office job.

Verdict: What it lacks in imagery and weight it makes up for in black comedy. A surprising close to *The Decalogue*, but all the more enjoyable because of it. 5/5

A Short Film About Killing
(Krotki Film O Zabijaniu, 1988)

Cast: Miroslaw Baka (Jacek), Jan Tesarz (Taxi Driver), Krzysztof Globosz (Piotr), Artur Barcis (Young Man)

Crew: Direction Krzysztof Kieslowski, Screenplay Krzysztof Kieslowski & Krzysztof Piesiewicz, Music Zbigniew Preisner, Editing Ewa Small, Cinematography Slawomir Idziak, Feature film, 85 minutes

Background: Kieslowski always knew that *Decalogue 5* would be made into a feature-length version. But when the film-maker sat down with Piesiewicz to write *A Short Film About Killing*, public debate on the death penalty was not allowed at that time. Kieslowski nonetheless went ahead with the screenplay because it's "wrong no matter why you kill, no matter whom you kill and no matter who does the killing," he reasoned. He also wanted to articulate his experience of the Polish existence, "a world which is quite terrible and dull, a world where people don't have pity for each other, a world where they hate each other, a world where they not only don't help each other, but get in each other's way. A world where they repel each other. A world of people living alone." *A Short Film About Killing* is all of this. And so much more.

An American once told Kieslowski that the murder scene (in which Jacek throttles, beats with a stick and then bashes in the head of the taxi driver) is the longest ever committed to film. It takes seven and a half terrible minutes. Despite the length (and despite problems Kieslowski was having getting "blood" to run from the pipes under the blanket that was covering what was supposed to be the taxi driver's head - resulting in the crew suggesting the unpopular actor's head itself be used!), it was the state execution scene - which last just five minutes towards the end of the film - which was far more upsetting. A shoot set for one morning had to be delayed until the next day after a traumatic rehearsal. "The sight of the execution is simply unbearable," the director explained. "Even if it's only pretence." And even though only pretence, the end result was so affecting that after *A Short Film About Killing* was released (by which time debate had commenced on the subject of state executions in Poland), it helped contribute significantly to the anti-capital punishment argument. In 1989, the year after the film's completion, a new Polish government suspended all executions for five years.

Comment: Unlike its companion piece, *A Short Film About Killing* differs very little from its *The Decalogue* original. But, like *A Short Film About Love*, it opens and closes with alternative scenes and shots. Here, three opening images are designed to both unsettle the viewer while simultaneously setting the film's unpleasant tone: a cluster of barely discernible beetles, a dead rat in putrid water and a cat hanging by its neck (this last image foreshadows both Jacek's and the taxi driver's violent deaths).

It doesn't get any more palatable. Warsaw and its surroundings are shown in a very specific, visually repulsive way. Kieslowski accredited this idea to his trusted cinematographer Idziak, who made a selection of around 600 green filters for various set-ups to create a cruel and alienating landscape. It's a method more noticeably disturbing when seen in the cinema than on our television screens because convention dictates that our experience of what we see on the big screen is at least visually pleasing. In the cinema, we become more sensitive to ugliness. Added to this, Idziak worked with his trademark shoulder-mounted camera. Barely discernible on television, on the cinema screen this adds to a feeling of nervousness and nausea.

Idziak's filters also created an interesting technical effect: look closely and you'll see a shadow that seems to surround the action, particularly when watching the feature-length version of this on TV. Without going into technical details, this is basically to do with the copying process and the fact that contrast increases on television, so that what is light becomes lighter and what is dark, darker. Kieslowski described it as "an awful effect," but perhaps that's the point. Technically it's a fault. It's not supposed to be there. But stylistically it has the same effect as all of Kieslowski's beloved windows - we're constantly reminded that we're looking at the action, one step removed. What's more, the effect gives the audience the peculiar impression that it's peering into a hole, looking down into the nadir of humanity.

Scenes which appear in *A Short Film About Killing* and not in *Decalogue 5* add characterisation (the taxi driver's lottery visit, Jacek's interaction with the English-speaking tourist and his rebuttal of the gypsy and her cursing of him, Piotr's celebration at passing his law exam) or gruesome details perhaps unacceptable to television viewers (Jacek's rope initially going round the taxi driver's mouth rather than his neck, the taxi driver's false teeth falling out, the state executioner's struggle to correctly blindfold a struggling Jacek). The main difference, however, is a scene which gives Jacek a motive for the killing. After he has killed the taxi driver he returns to his girlfriend, Beata, who turns out to be the vegetable seller the taxi driver was leering at earlier. As she realises with growing horror what has happened, he says: "You wanted to go somewhere. Now we can drive anywhere you want."

Overall, *A Short Film About Killing* offers us more of Jacek's point of view than *5*, which is an exploration of Piotr's reasoning against capital punishment. The lawyer begins and ends *5*, and Kieslowski cuts to his argument throughout. *A Short Film About Killing* offers us not just a critique of the death penalty but also a litany of alienation, a spectacle of urban rubbish and a world of cruelty and despair.

Images: The manner of Jacek's death is invoked not just by the opening image of the hanged cat, but also by a plastic head that hangs from the taxi driver's rear-view mirror as a talisman. The boy's fate is also foreshadowed when, just before he enters the cinema, he is seen behind a barred door.

See Also: Decalogue 5.

Verdict: A statement against ugliness in both moral and aesthetic dimensions. Powerful enough to have direct political impact in the suspension of Poland's death penalty. 5/5

A Short Film About Love
(Krotki Film O Milosci, 1988)

Cast: Grazyna Szapolowska (Magda), Olaf Lubaszenko (Tomek), Stefania Iwinska (Landlady)

Crew: Direction Krzysztof Kieslowski, Screenplay Krzysztof Kieslowski & Krzysztof Piesiewicz, Cinematography Witold Adamek, Feature film, 87 minutes

Background: At the time of making *The Decalogue*, there were two sources of financing available to Polish film-makers. The first was Polish TV and the second was Poland's Ministry of Arts and Culture. Kieslowski approached the Ministry, offering to make them two feature films on the cheap drawn from *The Decalogue* stories. He stipulated that one of them had to be number 5 (surprise!), but the ministry could choose the other. It chose 6 and *A Short Film About Love* was born.

Kieslowski was having problems with casting and left things until the last minute. He and Grazyna Szapolowska had not parted on the best of terms after *No End*, and she was offered the role just three days before shooting began. Only after she accepted could they cast Olaf Lubaszenko as Tomek.

During rehearsals Szapolowska expressed reservations over the script. She claimed that it needed a "story," and Kieslowski gave way to female intuition. With Piesiewicz he came up with the alternative ending in which Magda visits Tomek on his return from hospital. As she looks through the telescope and 'sees' an earlier scene of her crying, she imagines being comforted by Tomek. Kieslowski liked this ending, not only because it left possibilities open (unlike the closure of the TV version), but also because it reminded the film-maker of the ending of *Camera Buff*, where Filip turns his camera on himself.

It was a memorable shoot for the director. To start with, it was a night shoot. The crew would arrive at 10pm at a dark suburban estate and shoot for six hours or so. It was bitterly cold. To create what was essentially two rooms on screen, Kieslowski and his crew had to find 17 different interiors. For the scenes looking down from Tomek's bedroom into Magda's apartment they also had to build a tower about 60 metres away from the house that was serving as Magda's apartment from which they could film. Kieslowski and cinematographer Witold Adamek would hole themselves up in the tower where a microphone and speaker system was rigged up so the film-maker could communicate with his actress across the block: to move her left leg a little higher, to spill the milk or pick up the cards. Sometimes the microphone failed and Kieslowski found himself shouting directions in order to be heard. "All through that week I had a really acute sense of idiocy, of the complete absurdity of my profession."

Comment: Like its companion piece, *A Short Film About Killing*, this too could be subtitled *A Short Film About Loneliness*. Tomek is an orphan. He's obsessed with Magda, who is introduced to us (via Kieslowski's lens as if WE were the ones spying on her) playing - notably - solitaire. She eats alone. He eats to accompany her, but they are separated by a courtyard. Tomek's landlady meanwhile, watches television on her own and later confides to Magda that she's afraid to be alone in the house. These are our two main protagonists and the bit player.

But this is also *A Short Film About Pain*. When Tomek asks his landlady why people cry, one of the explanations she gives includes: "when they can't take it anymore." She tells him how her son lessened pain by creating a physical pain elsewhere (with an iron on his chest). Tomek goes to his room and, seeing Magda sobbing at her kitchen table after an argument with one of her boyfriends, closes his eyes and stabs a pair of scissors between alternate fingers in a game of 'chance.' Finally he punctures a finger and shares a silent communion of pain with Magda. Similarly, after he receives the black eye and confesses his love to Magda, he goes up on the roof and uses the ice (instead of a hot iron) to distract himself from the pain of his humiliation.

Szapolowska's suggestion and the subsequent approach Kieslowski took to framing the central story removes the film from the straightforward realism that we see in 6. It differs far more from 6 than *A Short Film About Killing* does from 5.

Indeed, Kieslowski said he changed it in the cutting room more than any other film he'd ever made. *A Short Film About Love* opens with Magda in Tomek's room as he sleeps. She sits in the chair from which he spied on her. The story then takes place, as if in flashback from Tomek's point of view until the couple meet about two-thirds of the way through. Then the perspective shifts to Magda's. Up until that point, the film has been dealing exclusively with Tomek's feelings for Magda. With his departure, we see her feelings - guilt initially, but then compassion and friendship - and the film ends having completed the cycle, back at the opening scene. Magda is now the one looking through the telescope. This turns the film into a story of transgression, pain and reconciliation while *6* is merely a story of transgression and its consequences.

Images: Circles. The circular speaking hole in the post office window, the reflector in the window of Magda's apartment, the clock on her wall; all these images allude to the circular lens of the telescope, but also remind us that this film (shot through a round lens) will eventually come full circle when Magda takes her place at Tomek's telescope.

Hands. The opening shot introduces this theme, in which we see three hands: Magda's being prevented from touching Tomek's bandaged hand by his landlady's. This simultaneously intrigues us and sets up the premise (that of reaching out to someone and being prevented from doing so), and the outcome (a suicide attempt) which can be explored in flashback. Other images to do with hands include: Tomek's daring game of 'chance' with scissors, Tomek kissing his landlady's hand, close-ups of his fingers around the telescope, Magda noticing that Tomek has "such delicate hands" and teaching him how to caress hers. Also, Magda trails her finger through the spilt milk.

Colours: Red (Magda's work, her bedspread, the cloth on Tomek's telescope, his blood), White (the milk, the outfit worn by The Witness), Blue (Tomek's post office uniform, his sweater).

_ *See Also: Decalogue 6.*

Verdict: A career high point. 5/5

The Double Life Of Véronique
(La Double Vie De Véronique, 1991)

Cast: Irène Jacob (Veronika/Véronique), Philippe Volter (Alexandre), Wladyslaw Kowalski (Veronika's father), Claude Duneton (Véronique's father)

Crew: Direction Krzysztof Kieslowski, Screenplay Krzysztof Kieslowski & Krzysztof Piesiewicz, Cinematography Slawomir Idziak, Music Zbigniew Preisner, Feature film, 98 minutes

Story: Two identical girls are born, one (Veronika) in Poland and the other (Véronique) in France. Veronika is a musical girl who lives with her widowed father. On a trip to Krakow to visit her aunt she wins a competition to sing a haunting piece of music by Van den Budenmayer. Inadvertently caught in a political scuffle, she sees Véronique taking pictures from a tour bus. Despite suffering a mild heart attack following a rehearsal, Veronika goes ahead with the Van den Budenmayer concert and dies on stage after a sublime performance. At the time of Veronika's funeral, Véronique is making love to her boyfriend, during which she experiences a feeling of inexplicable loss. She decides to give up on her singing career and instead teaches music - including her beloved Van den Budenmayer - in a primary school. One day, a puppeteer visits the school and performs a story for the children involving a ballerina who seems to die during performance, after which she turns into a butterfly. Véronique is entranced and traces the puppeteer, Alexandre, to his shop, where she sees he also writes children's stories. Soon Véronique begins to receive mysterious objects in the post: a shoelace, an empty cigar box and a cassette of various sounds recorded in a station café. The latter leads her to Alexandre, who is waiting for her in the station café. After they make love, Alexandre finds the photos that Véronique took in Poland. For the first time Véronique sees her double, and is overwhelmed with emotion. Back at Alexandre's flat, Véronique discovers that not only has he made two puppets of her (because they are "damaged easily" during performances) but that he is writing a novel about two girls born on the same day in different countries whose lives eerily echo each other's. Véronique leaves him and returns to her father.

Background: The Double Life Of Véronique was Kieslowski's first film made outside Poland, and the director found the casting process in the West problematic. Andie Mac-Dowall was originally scheduled for the role (Kieslowski had been on the Cannes jury that awarded *sex, lies and videotape* the Palme d'Or), but the deal fell through and Kieslowski finally settled on a then-unknown Swiss actress, 24-year-old Irène Jacob. Kieslowski, who had been impressed by Jacob's brief appearance in Louis Malle's *Au Revoir Les Enfants*, was also touched by the actress' shyness when he screen-tested her. It was an inspired choice. After learning Polish for the role, Jacob went on to win the Best Actress award when the film premiered at Cannes.

Comment: Described by producer Leonardo de la Fuente as a "metaphysical thriller," *The Double Life of Véronique* is perhaps Kieslowski's most mystical film, his attempt to capture a soul on celluloid. "The film is about sensibility, presentiments and relationship which are difficult to name, which are irrational," said the director. "Showing this on film is difficult; if I show too much the mystery disappears; I can't show too little because then nobody will understand anything."

Veronika's early admission that she feels she is not alone in the world is paralleled by Véronique's late statement of exactly the same thing. Do the two women share the same soul? Certainly they share many defining traits aside from their physical appearance: both are sensuous singers with a weak heart and a predilection for Van den Budenmayer; both are affectionate to their widowed fathers; both have a habit of rubbing their lower eyelids with a ring; and both notice struggling old women who drop their bags. In Alexandre's puppet show we see the ballerina die (although we are told later that she merely breaks her leg) and be resurrected as a butterfly; later when he is describing his novel, the first of the two girls is burnt, warning the second one away from the hot stove. Is Véronique warned off singing by Veronika's death? Does Veronika die in order to release Véronique and let her fly? Nothing is certain in *The Double Life*

Of Véronique. Two girls, two stories, hundreds of interpretations.

Images: Elemental images of water, light, leaves. These indicate Veronika/Véronique's sensual nature. Véronique is introduced to us as a young girl; the voice-over (presumably her mother) tells her to look at the leaf she is holding, which ties Véronique with the elemental (at the end when she returns to her father's, she places her hand on the tree, re-rooting herself). The adult Veronika, meanwhile, is introduced to us singing in a downpour. As the other singers run for cover, only Veronika is left, and as she sings she turns her face up towards the falling rain with an expression of pure ecstasy. When she has her first heart attack, she is surrounded by dead leaves.

Recurring Images: Mirrors and glass. Kieslowski pulls out all the stops with mirrors, glass and various other instruments (a reflexive ball, a magnifying glass, a glass-topped coffin). At one point Véronique is woken up by a dancing light flickering over her face; when she goes to the window she sees a boy with a mirror and assumes he has been reflecting it into her room. But he goes inside, and the light is still flickering.

Colours: Cinematographer Slawomir Idziak, who used filters to such great effect in *A Short Film About Killing*, also employed them in *The Double Life Of Véronique*. This time though, he used a golden filter, and blue was deliberately eliminated from the film's colour spectrum, echoing Veronika/Véronique's essential warmth. Jacob is, for the large part, encased in red - bed linen, gloves, jumpers - just as she will later be in *Three Colours: Red*. When blue is used, it represents an object of Veronika/Véronique's love: the blue dress of Veronika's aunt, the sighting of Alexandre's reflection during the puppet show, his van.

Music: Although Preisner had worked with Kieslowski since *No End* and Van den Budenmayer (a fictitious 18th century Dutch composer invented by Kieslowski and scored by Preisner) had appeared along with the singer in *Decalogue 9*, *The Double Life Of Véronique* is the first of Kieslowski's films to feature music on an important textual level. When Kieslowski and Piesiewicz were writing *The Double Life Of Véronique* and looking for a profession for her, they thought of the girl from *Decalogue 9*, who chose elective heart surgery in order to be able to perform her beloved Van den Budenmayer. Véronique (and Veronika) was born. Both Veronika and Véronique love Van den Budenmayer. And it is Veronika's beautiful, deadly aria that audibly intertwines itself in both girls' lives.

And Another Thing: The American version features a different ending: in the original, Véronique drives to the house where her father is still living and pauses outside to touch a tree. Her father realises she's outside and raises his head from the bench where he's working. The American version features 1 minute of additional footage showing the father stepping outside the house, calling his daughter and Véronique running into his arms. Kieslowski shot the additional sequences after the film's premiere at the New York Film Festival in 1991, when he realised that the audience didn't understand the meaning of the original ending.

And Yet Another Thing: At one stage Kieslowski had the idea of making a different version of Véronique for each cinema, a "hand-made" film, as he called it. But although enough footage was gathered for this, the idea was jettisoned due to expense.

Verdict: Moving, mystical – magic! 5/5

The Three Colours Trilogy

Crew: Direction Krzysztof Kieslowski, Screenplay Krzysztof Kieslowski & Krzysztof Piesiewicz, Music Zbigniew Preisner, Three feature films, each approximately 90 minutes, 1993/4

Just as he provided the central premise for *The Decalogue*, it was Piesiewicz who originally suggested that Kieslowski make a film about the three concepts born out of the political context of the French Revolution: Liberty, Equality and Fraternity. As Kieslowski observed, "the West has implemented these three concepts on a political or social plane, but it's an entirely different matter on the personal plane." It was this personal level that Kieslowski was aiming towards, delving deeper into the human psyche than he had ever done before.

Having won international acclaim for *The Double Life Of Véronique*, Kieslowski had little problem in raising the cash for such an ambitious project, with most of the money coming from French institutions.

The writers worked as they always did. Piesiewicz supplied the ideas at every draft stage and Kieslowski wrote and rewrote the screenplay. Further comments were then invited from fellow Polish film-makers including Agnieszka Holland, Edward Klosinski and Edward Zebrowski, all of whom had served in this unofficial capacity for years. As with *The Decalogue*, the interpretation was to be resolutely contemporary. Each of the films started with a signifier of the present (*Three Colours: Blue* with a car's hydraulic pipe, *White* with a conveyor belt and *Red* with a telephone) but was to give way to a more spiritual, interior world.

Just as the French Revolution gave the *Three Colours Trilogy* its central conceit of Liberty, Equality and Fraternity, the *Trilogy* took its colours from the French flag. This gave the filmmakers not just a decorative look to the production, but room to work with emotional meanings as well. *Three Colours: Blue* was associated with melancholy; *White* with marriage and weddings; and *Red* with embarrassment and danger. Kieslowski chose his cinematographers carefully: as with *The Decalogue* he wanted to use three different cinematographers and decided to reward those who had helped make *The Decalogue* such a success. He chose long-term collaborator Slawomir Idziak (who had worked on early Kieslowski films, as well as *Decalogue 5*, *A Short Film About Killing* and *The Double Life Of Véronique*) for *Three Colours: Blue* because he thought that his expressionist camera could evoke a subjective state of mind; Edward Klosinski, who had shot *Decalogue 2* for *White*; and Piotr Sobocinski who had worked on the third and ninth parts of *The Decalogue* for *Red*. As always, film-making would be a collaborative experience for Kieslowski.

Given its complexity, the *Three Colours Trilogy* was made relatively quickly: according to Kieslowski - the whole thing from start to finish took less than three years. This was helped with allowing only a very short break between productions (indeed filming of *White* in Paris began the day after the *Blue* shoot wrapped) and by Kieslowski's habit of starting to shoot the next film while still editing its predecessor. The films premiered at Venice (September 1993), Berlin (February 1994) and Cannes (May 1994) respectively.

Three Colours: Blue
(Trois Couleurs: Bleu, 1993)

Cast: Juliette Binoche (Julie), Benôit Régent (Olivier), Florence Pernel (Sandrine), Charlotte Very (Lucille)

Crew: Direction Krzysztof Kieslowski, Screenplay Krzysztof Kieslowski & Krzysztof Piesiewicz, Cinematography Slawomir Idziak, Music Zbigniew Preisner, Feature film, 98 minutes

Concept: Liberty

Story: Julie loses her husband Patrice, a renowned composer, and their young daughter, Anna, in a car accident. After being unable to commit suicide with tablets stolen from the hospital, she decides to cut all ties with her past. She gives orders to clear and sell her country house, destroys Patrice's almost-finished score and sleeps with Olivier, her husband's collaborator, before setting up in an anonymous area of Paris. The only possession that she brings with her is a blue lamp from Anna's bedroom. Although she tries to forget, memories and snatches of music keep coming back to her, suggesting that she was co-author of the music that Patrice composed. Julie is befriended by Lucille, a neighbour and stripper whom other tenants in Julie's block want evicted. On answering a call to help Lucille at her strip club, Julie sees a documentary on television about Patrice, from which she learns that Olivier is planning to finish her husband's score (the copyist made a copy before Julie destroyed the original version) and also that Patrice had a mistress, Sandrine. Tracking Sandrine down, Julie learns that she is pregnant with Patrice's child. She helps Olivier finish the score for the concert and offers the family home, as well as Patrice's name, to Sandrine and her unborn son. In the final scene she makes love to Olivier and we see her smile faintly through her tears.

Background: Having worked so successfully with composer Preisner and cinematographer Idziak on *The Double Life Of Véronique*, the partnership became more essential to the making of this film than any of Kieslowski's previous ones. The score to *Blue*, which Preisner composed before shooting began, plays an even more integral part to *Blue* than it did in *The Double Life Of Véronique*, with the authorship of Patrice's music called into question and woven into the story (see below). Meanwhile Idziak's expressionist contribution was considered so eloquent that he was credited as screenplay collaborator.

Comment: In what is virtually a one-woman show, Juliette Binoche is hypnotic as Julie. Kieslowski delves deeper into the psyche than ever before, sharpening our attunement to Julie's inner life by indulging in a series of intimate shots from her point of view - an extreme close-up of Julie's eye, a lump of sugar sucking up the coffee, her reflection in a spoon as it sways back and forth. Similarly, fade-outs, traditionally used to represent time passing, here bring us back to exactly the same point in time at which the fade-out began. "The idea is to convey an extremely subjective point of view," explained Kieslowski. "That is, that time really does pass but for Julie, at a certain moment, it stands still...Not only does the music come back to her, but time stands still for a moment."

Having tried to live in liberty with nothing - no memory, desire, work, or relationships - Julie finds this an impossible existence to maintain. Various factors and events intrude upon her solitary existence - Olivier tracks her down, a nest of mice settles in her closet, the witness to the crash tracks her down and her neighbour befriends her. From her first tentative interactions with others (beginning with her helping put a sleeping tramp's head into a more comfortable position) to finding love, she finally achieves freedom. The last montage, set to the *Song For The Unification For Europe* (the finished version of Patrice's unfinished composition), consists of various aspects of Julie's life: Antoine, the witness of the crash, fingering Julie's crucifix which hangs around his neck; Julie's senile mother who appears to die; Lucille in the strip club; a scan of Sandrine's baby. The music accompanies Julie's epiphany, but it is the words, adapted from St. Paul's *First Letter To The Corinthians* (13: 1-3) that highlight the importance of love that Julie has now acknowledged:

"Though I speak with the tongue of angels, if I have not love, I am become as hollow brass. Though I have the gift of prophecy, and understand all mysteries and all knowledge, and though I have enough faith to move the mightiest of mountains, if I have not love, I am nothing. Love is patient, love is kind. It bears all things, it hopes all things. Love never fails. For prophecies shall fail, tongues shall cease, knowledge will wither away. And now shall abide faith, hope and love; but the greatest of these is love."

Julie's tears after making love with Olivier indicate a return to life (previously the housekeeper said that she was crying because Julie wasn't), but the fact that she is placed behind glass also suggests that she still has some way to go before she is fully revitalised.

Images: The Colour Blue. Blue permeates the film, and is used to create moods of melancholia and coldness, and to draw attention to the emotional associations conjured by certain objects in Julie's mind (e.g., the swimming pool, Anna's lamp).

Recurring Images: Reflections. Glass and other reflective surfaces here open up the theme of vision: the reflection of the doctor in the extreme close-up of Julie's eye when he tells her that her husband and daughter are dead; the television screen on which Julie watches the funeral; the rain reflected on her face (and illuminated with a blue light, representing the tears of sadness she is incapable of weeping) when she summons Olivier to her country home; the television screen at her mother's rest home. All of these represent Julie's inward journey - looking deep within herself - which ends with her approaching a clarity that allows her to continue living.

Music: Although Julie's way of expressing herself is through music, she is denied this emotional release due to the damage she may cause her dead husband's reputation. Having internalised her means of expression, every now and then a musical motif emerges out of the blue startling Julie and penetrating her solitude by refusing to go away. Musical notes often fill the screen visually, accompanying the musical notes heard on the soundtrack.

Look Out For: As Julie loiters in the hall of the courthouse for a glimpse of Sandrine, we see her poke her head into one of the courtrooms. There we see Karol from *White* in the middle of his divorce proceedings asking, "And what of equality?"

(Kieslowski's second *Trilogy* instalment tackles this concept.) Also look out for the old woman struggling to put a bottle in the recycling bin. Julie is so caught up in her own world that she doesn't even notice her - there are similar interludes in the subsequent two instalments, but the reaction of the protagonists differs.

Verdict: A symphony in blue, a masterpiece in melancholy. Brilliant. 5/5

Three Colours: White
(Trois Couleurs: Blanc, 1993)

Cast: Zbigniew Zamachowski (Karol), Julie Delpy (Dominique), Janusz Gajos (Mikolai), Jerzy Stuhr (Jurek)

Crew: Direction Krzysztof Kieslowski, Screenplay Krzysztof Kieslowski & Krzysztof Piesiewicz, Cinematography Edward Klosinski, Music Zbigniew Preisner, Feature film, 90 minutes

Concept: Equality

Story: White begins in Paris, in the law courts where Julie found Sandrine in *Blue*. Here Karol, a Polish hairdresser, is being humiliated by his French wife Dominique, who cites his sexual impotence as grounds for their divorce. After the case is heard, she leaves him nothing but a suitcase of his belongings, takes his passport and freezes their joint bank account. Karol is befriended by fellow weary Pole Mikolai, who agrees to smuggle Karol back into Poland in a trunk. Upon arriving in Warsaw, the suitcase is stolen and Karol is discovered by a group of angry thieves who beat him up and abandon him at a rubbish dump. Finally back at his brother's, Karol is no longer content to remain working at their humble hair salon, and scrambles to make a pot of cash in newly capitalist Poland. He becomes a security guard, then a currency dealer and, through shrewdness, amasses a fortune in a shady property deal and sets up a thriving business with Mikolai, who he tracks down at a bridge club. Karol's ultimate goal - to get Dominique back and to get his revenge - is realised in an elaborate plan when he stages his own death, acquiring a corpse from Russia ("These days you can buy anything") and depositing in the coffin a two franc coin that he has kept from the lowest point of his time in Paris. Dominique arrives for the funeral, only to find Karol - alive and sexually potent - in her hotel room. They finally consummate their marriage, but Karol leaves before the police arrive to arrest Dominique, who Karol has framed for his "murder." The film ends with Karol secretly visiting his ex-wife in prison where, upon gazing up at her with tears in her eyes, he sees Dominique would like to remarry him when she is released.

Background: It was obvious that Kieslowski would film one of the *Trilogy* instalments in his homeland and, although *White* starts off in Paris, the majority of the film is set in Poland. Zbigniew Zamachowski and Jerzy Stuhr are again cast as brothers in a black comedy (as in *Decalogue 10*).

Comment: "We understand the concept of 'equality,' that we all want to be equal," said Kieslowski. "But I think this is absolutely not true. I don't think anybody really wants to be equal. Everybody wants to be more equal. There's a saying in Polish: There are those who are equal and those who are more equal... That's what this film is about." The concept of equality here is not that of brotherhood, rather one of "getting even." Karol, whose humiliation begins with pigeon shit dropping on his shoulder, suffers involuntarily what Julie in *Blue* chooses to do. Systematically stripped of his possessions, he endures a public airing of his impotence (including when he calls Dominique up, only to hear her ecstatic moans while making love to someone else; to add insult to injury the public phone steals his money!), the taking of his passport, the cutting of his credit card in two (wincing visibly as it happens, the references to his impotence are obvious even to this hapless Pole!) and is finally sent underground (literally) when Dominique sets fire to their salon's curtains and informs the police it was an act of revenge by Karol. His utter humiliation propels him to proving himself more equal. Even when he has achieved it, lured Dominique to Poland, set a trap to frame her and consummated their love, he says of her moans during orgasm that she moaned louder when he overheard her on the phone.

But with Karol's final revenge, it seems that love can return to them at last. In this respect, *White* continues the theme that *Blue* set: the need to acknowledge the past to be able to let go of it and to proceed with the present. But Karol and Dominique are now both caught in his trap - in love but unable to be together.

Images: The colour white. White is, of course, virginal. It is also connected with weddings and we see two flashbacks (or perhaps flashforwards) of Karol and Dominique's wedding. White is also cold, and Dominique's cold and aloof manner towards Karol is echoed not only by her alabaster white skin (emphasised by blood red lipstick), but also in the bust that Karol steals from France and brings back to Poland with him. At one point the bust is so aligned with Dominique in his mind that he kisses it. White is also the colour of the pigeon shit that drops on Karol's suit and the toilet bowl in which he vomits after the court case. In Poland, it is the colour of the gulls circling the rubbish dump where Karol is deposited (and joyously sighs, "Jesus. Home at last!"), the colour of the wintry landscape and the ice upon which Mikolai and Karol drunkenly skate. The screen also fades out to white when Karol and Dominique finally consummate their love.

Recurring Images: Reflections. Karol looks at his reflection in a glass-framed icon of Madonna and child when he has successfully completed the first part of his shady deal in acquiring a small plot of prime real estate.

Look Out For: Julie from *Blue*, briefly poking her head into the courtroom where Karol and Dominique are fighting it out (although her interruption is not at the same point in the proceedings as it was in *Blue*!). Also the old man, trying to put his glass bottle into the recycling bin. Karol smiles ruefully to himself when he sees someone as impotent as he is, someone else having trouble getting it up and in, as it were. Perhaps this man is even worse off than he is.

Music: Just as the acting alternates between comic timing and emotional resonance, so does Preisner's music, highlighting the former with a tango and romantic piano and the latter with a more plaintive oboe or clarinet. The tango was an inspired choice. Not only because musically it expresses romantic longing, while physically the dance is performed with the man choreographing the couple's movements, but also because the first few notes replicate those of the James Bond theme tune. As Karol dives into a world of bodyguards, eavesdroppers and guns, we think of Agent 007!

Verdict: Kieslowski takes you by surprise (again) with this brilliantly paced, sly black comedy. A perfect central interlude to the *Trilogy*. 5/5

Three Colours: Red
(Trois Couleurs: Rouge, 1994)

Cast: Irène Jacob (Valentine), Jean-Louis Trintignant (Joseph Kern), Jean-Pierre Lorit (Auguste), Frédérique Feder (Karin)

Crew: Direction Krzysztof Kieslowski, Screenplay Krzysztof Kieslowski & Krzysztof Piesiewicz, Cinematography Piotr Sobocinski, Music Zbigniew Preisner, Feature film, 99 minutes

Concept: Fraternity

Story: Valentine, a warm and open young model living in Geneva, is struggling with a possessive boyfriend who is always abroad. Her neighbour, Auguste, is about to take an exam to become a judge. Their paths nearly cross but never quite do. One evening, Valentine accidentally runs over a dog and, on finding its cantankerous owner indifferent, takes the dog home and cares for it herself. When it is better, the dog runs back to its home leading Valentine to discover its owner eavesdropping on his neighbours' telephone conversations. She leaves in distress. Valentine's reaction causes the old man - a former judge, Joseph Kern - to shop himself to the police. His case makes the newspapers and, on reading about the scandal Valentine rushes back to the judge's home to tell him that she was not responsible for his denouncement. In their ensuing conversation he encourages her to take the ferry for her upcoming trip to England. Kern then accepts an invitation to one of Valentine's fashion shows and after the show Valentine guesses the judge's history - which has obvious parallels to Auguste's life. Valentine and Auguste (who has passed his law exam and witnessed his girlfriend making love to another man) board the same ferry but it capsizes in a huge storm. There are only a handful of survivors: Auguste, Valentine, Olivier and Julie from *Blue* as well as Karol and Dominique from *White*.

Background: After making the first two instalments in France (where most of the money for the *Trilogy* came from) and Poland (Home, Sweet Home!), it took a while to decide where to set and film the third. In the end, Kieslowski settled upon Switzerland because he wanted to film in another French-speaking country. However, it turned out that Geneva proved to be "exceptionally unphotogenic" and with no uniformity or character to it. Much of the action is set inside anyway, but cinematographer Piotr Sobocinski brought coherence to the film through his structuring of *Red* as an intricate play of recurring and reflecting images connecting three people - two of which echo each other from different periods of time. The part was written specifically for Irène Jacob because she had so impressed the director when they worked together on *The Double Life Of Véronique*.

Comment: Kieslowski described *Red* as being his most personal film - the closest he thought film could get to literature (a far superior medium, in his opinion). Its theme, fraternity, is, like the theme of equality in *White*, at first tackled obliquely - a retired judge eavesdropping on his homosexual, drug-dealing neighbours. However, it is the judge's connection with Valentine that opens the film up into a wider frame. "*Red* is really about whether people aren't, by chance, sometimes born at the wrong time," said the director.

Kieslowski decided that the film would be made in the conditional mood: what might have happened had Kern been born forty years later. Kern admits to Valentine that she would perhaps have been the right woman for him, although note that everything that happens to Auguste happened to the older judge (the book falling open at the right page for his exam, seeing his lover in bed with another man). Is Auguste a person in his own right? Or is he merely just an echo of Kern? And is Kern more than what he appears to be? Kieslowski likened him to a chess player; others have compared him to a God-like figure. He certainly seems omniscient, and perhaps has more of hand in bringing Valentine and Auguste together than he lets on.

Ultimately though, it is this misanthropic recluse that brings the naive model wisdom, while she reintroduces him to compassion and, of course, a new notion of fraternity. At the end, as Valentine finally connects with Auguste, we see the elderly judge smile as he looks out through his (broken) window. His encounter with Valentine has enabled him to reconnect with the world and unlike Julie in *Blue*, he is not separated from it by glass.

Images: The colour red. Red is passion, danger, warmth and also the colour of blood, a life force. The colour is emphasised not through lighting or filters, but instead the film is built up through the use of red objects: red clothes; the dog's leash; Auguste's car; the cherries on a slot machine (playing it shows Valentine is a believer in chance!); red paper wrapped around some pear brandy; and Valentine's ticket. The examples are endless. Try and list them for yourself - it's impossible.

Phones, surveillance, cameras. Human contact is reduced to technological connections, extending the possibilities of error and missed opportunities. This is a theme which is set in Kieslowski's virtuoso opening sequence, which begins with a hand dialling a phone number. The camera traces the call via the plug socket, down through the cable and under the sea only to end up with a busy tone, flashing red. This is a film, after all, about missed connections. Auguste doesn't have an answering machine and therefore misses the call from Karin (who makes her living giving weather reports over the phone) at an important moment. Valentine's phone - and her conversations with her lover - are a source of constant frustration, while the judge bugs his neighbours' telephone conversations in an intriguing take on the meaning of fraternity. The biggest missed connection of all is Valentine and the judge, who confesses to her after his visit to the fashion show that she is perhaps the 'right' woman he never met.

Recurring Images: When Valentine parts with the judge after the fashion show, they join the palms of their hands on each side of her car window, just as Witek did with his girlfriend as she left on the train in the second section of *Blind Chance*.

Reflections/windows. Valentine is seen behind her car windscreen; there is much looking through windows; Auguste sees his reflection in the window when, like Tomek in *Decalogue 6* and Karol in *White*, he sees the object of his affection making love with another.

Chance. The whole film is launched with a chance incident, with Valentine running over a dog. And it is concluded with a storm, an event beyond the control of mortals resulting in a fatalistic meeting between Valentine and Auguste.

Music: For *Red*, Preisner composed a haunting bolero. It couldn't get more appropriate. Filled with romantic longing, a bolero also takes on the form of two separate musical motifs that intertwine to form a coherent whole. Which is exactly what Valentine and Kern/Auguste seem to do.

Look Out For: Van den Budenmayer, whose portrait is seen on the cover of a record that the judge has. Also the woman who struggles to put a glass in the recycling bin. It is Valentine, Kieslowski's most generous and pure-hearted heroine, who finally comes to the aid of the stooped old woman. Finally, of course, Olivier and Julie from *Blue*, and Karol and Dominique from *White*.

Verdict: A fitting climax, but personally I find the 'What if?' mood degenerating slightly into 'So What?' But brilliantly executed, brilliantly acted and there's no denying the formal chemistry between Trintignant and Jacob. 4/5

Epilogue

It was at the premiere of *Red* at the Cannes Film Festival that Kieslowski announced his retirement. He told a group of stunned American journalists that he now had enough money to keep himself in cigarettes and, rather than subject himself to the strain and bother of making films, he would prefer to retire to his house in the country and read novels. Perhaps he would watch a little television. But never would he go to the movies. The film director had lost his patience for film-making. He wanted to lead a normal life.

Like all of Kieslowski's public statements, it was taken with a pinch of salt by those who knew him. He had long hidden his passions behind a mask of sardonic detachment and self-proclaimed pessimism and it wasn't too long before news leaked out that he was indeed working on a new trilogy with Piesiewicz, entitled *Heaven*, *Hell* and *Purgatory*.

But he was not to see it through. In March, 1996, having already suffered a stroke, Kieslowski refused offers from specialists in Paris and New York and from two specialised open-heart surgery centres in Poland, and instead checked himself in for elective heart surgery in his local hospital. He was an ordinary Pole, he insisted. No special treatment. Sadly, his attempts to live an ordinary life were tragically short-lived. Kieslowski died after surgery on March 13, less than two years after announcing his 'retirement.'

Did he stop making movies because he knew he was going to die? Or did he believe he had already said everything he had to say and had lost the will to live? Kieslowski once said that he believed people died simply when they could no longer go on living.

We shall never know for sure whether he planned to return to directing. Irène Jacob, who remained in close contact with Kieslowski, later said that he only planned to write and oversee production - as he had originally intended with *The Decalogue*, he would hand directing duties for each film over to a different young director.

In the meantime, one of the director's favourite actors, Jerzy Stuhr (*Camera Buff, Decalogue 9, Three Colours: White*) has unearthed an old Kieslowski script, *Big Animal*. Stuhr stars in and directs this bizarre (and, it seems, very un-Kieslowski-like) tale of a bank employee who brings home a camel he finds on the streets of his home town. The film is dedicated to the late director.

So Kieslowski may be dead, but his spirit (and screenplays) live on. The latest news is that Anthony Minghella (writer/ director of *The English Patient* and *The Talented Mr Ripley*) is to produce *Heaven*, the first chapter of the trilogy Kieslowski was working on when he died. Miramax, which did such a superb job of distributing Kieslowski's films in America and bringing the director's work to the attention of a whole new audience, is to fund it. We shall just have to wait and see what it will do with his legacy. Cate Blanchett and Giovanni Ribisi have been lined up to star in *Heaven*, which follows a Scottish woman who moves to Tuscany and falls in love with a young Italian. German Tom Tykwer is to direct. Tykwer is indeed young, but I can't help feeling trepidation at the thought of what someone who directed *Run Lola, Run* (essentially a jumped-up video game) might do to the nuances of a Kieslowski script. Just like Witek in *Blind Chance*, Lola did a lot of running, but that was pretty much it.

Kieslowski, forever the solitary smoker observing the foibles of human behaviour, offered so much more.

Reference Materials

Books

There are lots of books in Polish, French and - bizarrely - Italian, but not much in English, it seems. Here's what there is:

Kieslowski On Kieslowski edited by Danusia Stok, UK: Faber & Faber, 1994, £12.99, ISBN 0571173284. Dive into Kieslowski's world where the glass is not just half empty, it's also cracked AND you'll cut your lip on it if you're not careful. The phlegmatic film-maker talks about his films and offers an entertainingly sardonic take on existence. This is invaluable due to the lack of interviews conducted in English with him (you may recognise large chunks of it in this book!) Essential.

The Three Colours Trilogy by Geoff Andrews, UK: BFI, 1998, £8.99, ISBN 0851705693. Excellent detailed analysis of Kieslowski's last works, with a bit on background and also a transcript of an interview. Personal, sympathetic and well-written.

Double Lives, Second Chances: The Cinema Of Krzysztof Kieslowski by Anette Insdorf, US: Hyperion, 1999, £16.99, ISBN 0786865628. One of Kieslowski's translators who became his friend offers a reasonably accessible academic introduction to his work. Excellent on background and well-written, she occasionally deconstructs a little too far for my liking. Very much like...

Lucid Dreams: The Films Of Krzysztof Kieslowski edited by Paul Coates, UK: Flicks Books, 1999, ISBN 0948911638. A collection of essays from British, American, Canadian and Polish scholars. For the hard core. Only to be tackled wearing a black polo neck and tortoiseshell glasses (goatee beard for men optional). On the plus side, it contains the transcript of one of Kieslowski's last interviews.

Krzysztof Kieslowski by Anne Jackal UK: Longman, 2000, £10.99, ISBN 0582437377. Scheduled to be published one month before this. Stealing my thunder.

Screenplays

Decalogue: The Ten Commandments by Krzysztof Kieslowski & Krzysztof Piesiewicz, UK: Faber & Faber 1991, £12.99, ISBN 0571144985

Three Colours Trilogy: Blue, White, Red by Krzysztof Kieslowski & Krzysztof Piesiewicz, UK: Faber & Faber, 1998, £12.99, ISBN 0571178928

Videos/DVD

Camera Buff, New Yorker Films, 1994, $79.99, VHS NTSC, ASIN: 6303139655

No End, New Yorker Films, 1996, $26.99, VHS NTSC, ASIN: 6302993202

The Decalogue, Image Entertainment, 2000, $70.00, DVD, ASIN: 6302993202

Dekalog – The Ten Commandments part 1-5 (two cassettes), Artificial Eye, 1988, £22.99, PAL VHS, ASIN: B00004CM87

Dekalog – The Ten Commandments part 6-10 (two cassettes), Artificial Eye, 1988, £22.99, PAL VHS, ASIN: B00004CM8A

A Short Film About Killing, Tartan Video, 1995, £15.99, PAL VHS, TVT1091

A Short Film About Love, Tartan Video, 1995, £15.99, PAL VHS, TVT1092

The Double Life Of Véronique, Tartan Video, 1993, £15.99, PAL VHS, ASIN: B00004CN1H

Three Colours: Blue, Artificial Eye, 1994, £15.99, PAL VHS, ASIN: B00004CO4G

Three Colours: White, Artificial Eye, 1994, £15.99, PAL VHS, ASIN: B00004CP3L

Three Colours: Red, Artificial Eye, 1995, £15.99, PAL VHS, ASIN: B00004CPTM

Krzysztof Kieslowski: I'm So-So..., Totally absorbing documentary directed by Krzysztof Wiersbicki, First Run Features, 1995, $29.99, VHS NTSC, ASIN: 6305269416

Websites

Kieslowski homepage - with links to other articles: http://www-personal.engin.umich.edu/~zbigniew/Kieslowski/kieslowski2.html

With testimonials, essays and links: http://homepage.iprolink.ch/~gujski/KWN/kwnindex.html

Great introductory resource for fans of the director that includes pictures, a list of books and articles, and links: http://www.petey.com/kk/

Kieslowski's thoughts on a poem that encapsulates *Red*: http://www.mty.itesm.mx/dcic/centros/cinema16/tres_colores/texto/kieslowsky/kieslowsky.html

"We live in the world lacking idea on itself." Long essay by Tadeusz Miczka: http://www.arts.uwaterloo.ca/FINE/juhde/micz971.htm

Derek Malcolm on A Short Film About Killing: http://www.filmunlimited.co.uk/Century_Of_Films/Story/0,4135,140594,00.html

The immensely quotable Kieslowski: http://www.tiac.net/users/write/kieslowski/kieslowski.htm

Links and their site contents: http://magellan.excite.com/entertainment/movies/directors_and_producers/last_names_k_m/kieslowski_krzysztof

The Essential Library

Enjoyed this book? Then try some other titles in the Essential library.

New This Month:

> **Jane Campion** by Ellen Cheshire
>
> **Krzysztof Kieslowski** by Monika Maurer

New Next Month:

> **David Cronenberg** by John Costello
>
> **Slasher Movies** by Mark Whitehead

Also Available:

Film:

> **Woody Allen** by Martin Fitzgerald
> **Jackie Chan** by Michelle Le Blanc & Colin Odell
> **The Brothers Coen**
> by John Ashbrook & Ellen Cheshire
> **Film Noir** by Paul Duncan
> **Terry Gilliam** by John Ashbrook
> **Heroic Bloodshed** edited by Martin Fitzgerald
> **Alfred Hitchcock** by Paul Duncan
> **Stanley Kubrick** by Paul Duncan
> **David Lynch** by Michelle Le Blanc & Colin Odell
> **Steve McQueen** by Richard Luck
> **Brian De Palma** by John Ashbrook
> **Sam Peckinpah** by Richard Luck
> **Vampire Films** by Michelle Le Blanc & Colin Odell
> **Orson Welles** by Martin Fitzgerald

TV:

Doctor Who by Mark Campbell

The Simpsons by Peter Mann

Books:

Stephen King by Peter Mann

Noir Fiction by Paul Duncan

Available at all good bookstores at £2.99 each, or send a cheque to: **Pocket Essentials (Dept KK), 18 Coleswood Rd, Harpenden, Herts, AL5 1EQ, UK** Please make cheques payable to 'Oldcastle Books.' Add 50p postage & packing for each book in the UK and £1 elsewhere.

US customers can send $5.95 plus $1.95 postage & packing for each book to **Trafalgar Square Publishing, PO Box 257, Howe Hill Road, North Pomfret, Vermont 05053, USA**. tel: 802-457-1911, fax: 802-457-1913, e-mail: tsquare@sover.net

Customers worldwide can order online at **www.pocketessentials.com**, **www.amazon.com** and at all good online bookstores.